A GUIDE
TO CARING FOR
AND COPING WITH
AGING PARENTS

A GUIDE TO CARING FOR AND COPING WITH AGING PARENTS

John Gillies

THOMAS NELSON PUBLISHERS
Nashville

Published in Nashville, Tennessee, by Thomas Nelson, Inc., Publishers and distributed in Canada by Lawson Falle, Ltd., Cambridge, Ontario.

Scripture verses are from the Revised Standard Version of the Bible, copyrighted 1946, 1952, © 1971, 1973.

Excerpt from "Portrait of the Artist as a Prematurely Old Man" by Ogden Nash copyright © 1934 by The Curtis Publishing Company. First appeared in the *Saturday Evening Post*. By permission of Little, Brown and Company.

Excerpt from "Portrait of the Artist as a Prematurely Old Man" reprinted by permission of Curtis Brown, Ltd. Copyright © 1934, 1959 by Ogden Nash. (World, excluding the United States and Canada.)

Library of Congress Cataloging in Publication Data

Gillies, John, 1925-
  A guide to caring for and coping with aging
parents.

  1. Parents, Aged—United States. 2. Parents,
Aged—United States—Family relationships.
3. Aged—Health and hygiene. I. Title.
HQ1064.U5G44   646.7′8   81-1138
ISBN 0-8407-5772-7   AACR2

Dedicated to the memory of
Katherine B. Tiffany,

professor of English at Wheaton College,
who first encouraged me to write,
and who finally completed her own writing
at the age of one hundred
at the Presbyterian Home
in Quarryville, Pennsylvania.

Contents

Contents

Contents

Contents

Introduction

Crabbed age and youth cannot live together;
Youth is full of pleasaunce,* age is full of care;
Youth like summer morn, age like winter weather;
Youth like summer brave, age like winter bare.
Youth is full of sport, age's breath is short;
Youth is nimble, age is lame;
Youth is hot and bold, age is weak and cold;
Youth is wild, and age is tame.
Age, I do abhor thee; youth, I do adore thee.

—William Shakespeare (1564–1616)
The Passionate Pilgrim

There is a new awareness of aging among us. Much is being written about the subject; government agencies are giving it attention; a national White House consultation has been held; and local seminars are being called. This is good and long overdue, for we are living longer and growing older.

In 1900, only 1 American out of 25 was over 65 years of age. Today, it's 1 out of 10.

Every day, approximately 5,000 Americans turn 65 and about 3,600 aged persons die. Thus, our older population increases by approximately 1,400 persons every day. It is projected that by the year 2000 there will be more than 30.6 million older persons in the United States, or 11.7 percent of our total population.

So much for statistics. What about the human side?

Most of our older people are still women. There are five times as many widows as widowers. Women have the highest poverty rate in the nation.

The nuclear family is disappearing—through divorce, mobility,

---

*"being pleased"

11

or smaller living areas—and this affects oldsters as well as youngsters.

Despite the good health and enthusiastic energy of most of the 23 million older Americans, at least 1 in 10 is unable to be totally independent, and 1 in 20 lives in some kind of institution. Furthermore, inflation affects the independent *and* the institutionalized—as well as the rest of us.

This book is written for those of us who are caught in the middle. You and I are likely in our forties or fifties; some call us the "sandwich generation."

We were the first generation to rear our children according to Dr. Spock. Our parents did not understand the new principles and permissiveness. Those children lived through the trauma and terror of the sixties. Dr. Amitai Etzioni says it was really a period of fifteen years—"a decade and a half of retreat from institutions, identity, directions, and commitment." Before it was over, we were as confused about our children as our parents were about all of us.

We survived, somehow. We began to contemplate future pleasure and leisure, began to live without constant confrontation and crisis. And having just arrived at this point in our lives, many of us now face new responsibilities and problems. We are caught in the middle, between youth and age; our generation gaps extend in both directions. Now we must become parents to our parents, and we are no more prepared for this new journey and experience than we were when we first became natural parents.

The circumstances of life and the new longevity already have forced some of us to assume this new role of parenting our parents. Others of us know we must prepare for it soon. In either case, parents and their middle-aged children must take time to realistically evaluate where we are, together, in this process of lengthened life. We must plan with love and understanding for the years that lie ahead.

This is not a technical book on gerontology, nor is it a book of advocacy for the rights of older Americans. Others have done this and continue to do this, and they are far better qualified than I to do so. This book is a record of *learned experiences,* a guide to coping with the new role of parenting and decision-making for older loved ones who suddenly require our help. I guess it's really a "how-we-did-it" book.

It contains the record of Anna and Paul, of whom you will be hearing much more. Anna is my mother. Paul is my father-in-law. At this writing, both are residents in nursing homes.

This book traces our confusion and our emerging convictions over a period of five years—first through perceptions of a developing problem, then through home care and retirement centers and debilitating accidents, and finally to long-term skilled and institutionalized care.

A Small Disclaimer

My wife, Carolyn, and I learned through necessity and urgency. If at times it sounds as though we found *the* answer for any given situation or problem, then I have recounted the experience badly. Sometimes we were lucky—or blessed.

We don't have all the answers. Far from it. In fact, we're still learning. In your own learning experience, I'm sure you will have other ideas and solutions you'll want to try.

As I write this, Anna and Paul are still alive. They are not physically ill, but they are severely handicapped. Carolyn and I do not know yet how the story will end—for them or for us.

During these past five years, Carolyn and I have been blessed by coming to know dozens of Americans inside and outside our family circles—some older, some younger, of different colors and cultures and persuasions.

Few of them are mentioned by name, but all have contributed to our experience and to this book.

1

Your Perspective on Aging

All the world's a stage,
And all the men and women merely players:
They have their exits and their entrances;
And one man in his time plays many parts,
His acts being seven ages . . .
Infant . . .
School-boy . . .
Lover . . .
Soldier . . .
Justice [Judge] . . .
Lean and slipper'd . . .
Last scene of all,
That ends this strange eventful history,
Is second childishness, and mere oblivion,
Sans teeth, sans eyes, sans taste, sans everything.

—William Shakespeare
As You Like It

One of the many books written about aging is *Nobody Ever Died of Old Age,* by Sharon Curtin.

That's only partially true, of course.

We die mostly from heart disease (and heart failure), cancer, circulatory problems, urinary infections, bronchitis, and accidents. Among the latter is the "cerebrovascular accident" (the CVA)—better known to us as "stroke," caused by hemorrhage, clot, sclerosis, or blockage of a blood vessel in the brain. Diabetes also kills many among the aging.

And yet, as Seneca claimed, old age itself is an incurable disease. Even if we live to be 150 in the twenty-first century, as some predict, there will be an end to earthly life.

Aging Within a Youth Culture

We begin to age as soon as we are born. This is evidenced by falling hair, failing eyesight and hearing, shrinking muscles, twisted joints, and wrinkled skin. The rate of change is affected by a variety of factors: where we live, how we eat, our heredity, and our work environment. Some people appear ancient at fifty-five. Others remain vivacious and clear of mind at ninety-five. Many people now question whether anyone should be pressured to retire at age sixty-five. It all depends.

Shakespeare first reminded us about the ages of life. It is good to remember that we progress from childhood through youth and middle age to maturity, and that we do so at our own particular, individual pace.

We must also distinguish between *senescence* and *senility*. Senescence is merely growing old, maturing, aging. Perhaps we can think of it as a kind of "ripening." *Senility*, on the other hand, describes a feebleness of body and mind, a deterioration that is often irreversible.

Too often we label people "senile" when they may be suffering from depression, nutritional deficiencies, tumors, infection, or even drug interactions. These kinds of conditions can be treated and helped.

Robert Browning wrote, "Grow old along with me, the best is yet to be." For hundreds of fortunate oldsters, Browning's promise has proved to be true. For them, there are still "golden years" at the end of life.

Life in later years can be happy and productive. We have too long been conditioned by advertising and the media that "young is beautiful." The hucksters abhor age, and it appears that we eagerly agree. We spend eight times as much on cosmetics as we do on public care for the aging.

Our Fantasy About Old Age

Bert Kruger Smith, author of *Aging in America*, admonishes us to discard at least four myths regarding older Americans.

First of all, she says, it is a myth that *older people cannot learn.* A folk saying puts it thus: "You can't teach an old dog new tricks."

But you can. Meaningful opportunities and stimuli for older citizens have demonstrated their potential for learning.

A second myth is that *sexual interest and activity is limited to the young.* God's gift of sexuality is not limited. The biblical characters of Abraham, Boaz, and David attest to this. The apostle Paul's advice to widows underscores this: "It is better to marry than to be aflame with passion" (1 Cor. 7:9).

To be sure, some live-in arrangements among older people are due more to economics than affection. While it was never true that two can live as cheaply as one, two unmarried people can collect larger Social Security checks if they remain "single" and pool their benefits.

Paul Young, my father-in-law, was about to be married for the third time (he was widowed twice) when he had his stroke. I am sure that his intentions, even at age eighty-three, were not merely platonic nor only spiritual. He wanted a companion and a wife. Paul enjoys the romantic courtship he sees on television; he's also often amused by the sexual innuendoes and implications.

I remember visiting Anna in her first nursing home. She was sitting near the nurses' station on that particular day when a shriveled-up male hobbled by, stopped in front of us, and asked, "Where can I find a woman?" Although my mother's speech and sense of orientation were beginning to fail, she replied with a twinkle in her eye, "So that's what you have on your mind!"

Many of the newer nursing home facilities encourage husbands and wives to share rooms whenever this is desired and possible. Many homes also provide visiting rooms, away from the public lounges, for those residents who want a more private setting for conversation and, I fully believe, for romance. You don't have to visit a nursing home very long before you'll notice some pairing off among the residents and even hear an occasional lovers' quarrel.

Smith points to a third myth—*older people do not want to work.* She insists that many physically able persons prefer to work beyond mandatory retirement age, not so much because of the income (important as that is in times of inflation) but because they need to feel needed and useful. Paul commuted between Florida and Ecuador well into his eighties. Until Anna broke a hip and could no longer walk and explore, she remained physically active even when her mind had ceased to function. Many groups are discovering the valuable contributions of time and skills older volunteer workers can provide.

The fourth myth Mrs. Smith cites is that *older people like to be helpless*. It is often hard for me to restrain myself from giving help, especially when a loved one is handicapped and a clear danger exists. Nevertheless, Smith reminds us that most older people, even those who are handicapped, prize whatever degree of independence is still available to them.

Other myths merit attention. Hugh Downs cites thirty "lies" about aging in his popular book (see "Resources" at end of chapter).

Not every older person is forgetful. Many do like to reminisce and many do tend to remember what was exciting and adventuresome in their youth, perhaps forgetting what happened yesterday. But many older people can still recite the Apostles' Creed, portions of Holy Scripture, or sing hymns from memory. Not a few older people make a living at professional acting, which requires the ability to learn and remember lines.

Older people are not necessarily happiest when they are with other older people. Many oldsters prefer to remain within familiar neighborhoods and shopping facilities, where a mix of ages exists. Churches and other groups can provide opportunities for bridging generation gaps and creating new and exciting links. Sometimes an older person requires the sense of comfort and security of being in the company of peers, but very few want this to be their only company.

Older people do not necessarily have all their personal and spiritual accounts settled. Some elderly people still harbor grudges and waste away with bitterness. Like the rest of us, they need to find forgiveness from friends, family, and God. They may even need to forgive themselves.

Beware the New Legends of Our Time

As we demythologize aging, however, let's not invent new myths.

One of these is the blind belief that the Browning notion of "the best is yet to be" applies to everyone past sixty-five. A vast institutional population would not agree—nor would their families.

Old isn't always beautiful. An old building may be a beautifully preserved historical landmark—or a tenement. A chair may be a highly polished and elegant antique—or a broken piece of junk. Beauty is always in the eye of the beholder, and remembering what *was* distorts what *is*. More than a million older people in the United States live in environments and situations that are devoid of hope, and for them old is not beautiful.

There was a recent example of this on public television. PBS aired a ninety-minute special called "Charlie Smith and the Fritter Tree" on its *Visions* series. Charlie was allegedly born in Liberia, brought to New Orleans, and sold as a slave. He gained his freedom and worked as a cowboy, bounty hunter, and con man. He was said to be the oldest living American. The program made Charlie into a kind of folk hero who was said to be 135 at the time the program was filmed. The real Charlie, looking older than any man should, lived and died in a Florida nursing home—legless, senile, and quite unaware of the fuss being made over him.

It is an ongoing myth that youth is best. Ponce de Leon sought his "fountain of youth" long ago, and we refuse to give up the search. The quest continues, led by well-meaning and well-motivated social workers and advocates.

I was thrilled with Artur Rubinstein's superb concert, given on his ninetieth birthday. I was amazed and pleased recently to hear Averell Harriman—at age eighty-seven—discuss international affairs with great lucidity. They and other fortunate ones like them are examples of perseverance and strength, but they are *not* examples of perpetual youth.

Perhaps our "social engineers" should be a trifle more cautious in suggesting that everyone be allowed to work or drive as long as he wishes or appears to be able; that little risk exists for worker, driver, or the rest of us; that the latter years are *always* "golden years" of creativity and wisdom. I wish the myths were fact.

In a workshop recently I used the word "senility" and was gently clobbered by a couple of people who said I should talk about "progressive deterioration" or "progressive dementia" instead. Apparently this is a way to attack "ageism" in our culture, just as others attack "sexism" in our language.

The word "senility" will be found in this book, used in its precise, medical meaning. (I prefer precision in words. "Sin," I think, is better than "social problem"; "racism" says more than "ethnocentricity.")

It's good that Bert Kruger Smith, Hugh Downs, and others help us to identify and discard the myths and lies that distort our perception of older people. But we are not ageless, and one of the risks of living is that some of us age faster than others; some of us deteriorate more quickly than others.

We do die daily—at least, parts of us do. We don't want to be reminded of our mortality, that there will be an end to life. Perhaps this is why strong, able older people don't really enjoy visiting deteriorating, handicapped older people.

Somehow we must come to terms with our own deterioration. We must find and maintain a perspective on aging if we are to help those who struggle for meaning, worth, and reality.

One of the most instructive Sunday school classes I ever attended was a class on Quaker beliefs, taught by eighty-five-year-old Mrs. McWhorter. During the class period, she would stop and say, "Now you may not agree with this, but it certainly makes you think." She enjoyed thinking and probing, and I suspect she took special delight in getting us to think and question and evaluate.

I'm blessed with many older friends—people in their seventies, eighties, and nineties.

Louise Wilson reads books and loves to discuss them and their ideas. Alvin Burger was a professional researcher and one of the most able organizers you could find; it was a privilege to work on committees with him. Harold Kilpatrick is a former boss; he and his wife, Zel, continue to win prizes for their gardens. Harold specializes in vegetables, Zel in flowers—particularly irises. Both should get prizes for their spirited involvement in church, community, and cultural activities.

It has been a privilege to visit and chat with people such as Mrs. "Mac," Louise, Alvin, Harold, and Zel. I've never been aware of generation gaps or any other kind of gaps, other than the limitation of time and geography.

But it's much different with older people who are failing in mobility, in sight, in hearing, and most sadly, in mind. These are the kinds of older people this book is about.

The time has come to meet two such people—the two who made Carolyn and me parents again.

Resources—Chapter 1

Many books will be mentioned as resources throughout this book. You may want to purchase some of these. However, remember that your public library is your source for these and other books. If your local library does not have a particular title, you may be able to secure it through an "inter-library loan" service.

● The magazine *Issues* was once published by the United Church of Christ. Perhaps your church subscribed. There may be copies in a nearby seminary library. Look for the Summer, 1977, issue entitled "Growing Old: A Cause for Rejoicing." It is excellent.

● There's a song in *Jacques Brel Is Alive and Well and Living in Paris* called "Old Folks." John Denver has made a haunting recording of it. This could be a discussion starter for this chapter or the one on planning for funerals. Perhaps you recall that Brel, the Belgian singer, died in 1978 at the age of forty-nine.

● You might want to read *The Gin Game* by D. L. Coburn. It's not for everyone, as it contains some raw and raucous language. Hume Cronyn and Jessica Tandy, a husband-and-wife acting team, did the play on Broadway. It deals with the loneliness and confusion of aging in an institution.

● The Metropolitan Life Insurance Company publishes many public service booklets. You might be able to borrow an older booklet entitled "When Our Parents Get Old." Check with your local office.

● Several of the following books would make a good basis for a group discussion.

Anderson, Margaret. *Your Aging Parents.* St. Louis: Concordia, 1979.
Bromley, D. B. *The Psychology of Human Ageing.* New York: Penguin Books, rev. ed., 1974. Heavy reading at times but a classic textbook.

Butler, R. N. *Why Survive? Being Old in America.* New York: Harper and Row, 1975.

Calhoun, Richard B. *In Search of the New Old (Redefining Old Age in America).* New York: Elsevier, 1978.

Cohen, Stephen Z. *The Other Generation Gap.* Chicago: Follett, 1978.

Downs, Hugh. *Thirty Dirty Lies About Old.* Niles, Ill.: Argus Communications, 1979.

Freese, Arthur S. *The End of Senility.* New York: Arbor House, 1978.

Myerhoff, Barbara. *Number Our Days.* New York: E. P. Dutton, 1979. This is a perceptive and amusing study of a Jewish community in California.

Otten, June and Florence D. Shelley. *When Your Parents Grow Old.* New York: Funk and Wagnall's, 1976.

Silverstone, Barbara, and Helen Kandel Hyman. *You and Your Aging Parent.* New York: Pantheon, 1976.

Smith, Bert Kruger. *Aging in America.* Boston: Beacon Press, 1973.

2

Paul Lewis Young

Nobody loves life like an old man.
—Sophocles (496?–406 B.C.)

The telephone rang around two in the morning. Middle-of-the-night calls always stir up the adrenalin.

It was a doctor from the St. Paul Ramsey Hospital in St. Paul, Minnesota. Paul Young had suffered a stroke earlier that evening, he said, but it wasn't known yet how serious it was. Carolyn, one of Paul's two daughters, was being asked to give permission to make whatever tests were necessary. She quickly consented.

Carolyn called her sister, Esther, in Maryland, and made plans to fly immediately to Minneapolis-St. Paul, where she stayed for several days. Esther and I rearranged our own schedules and were able to visit Paul ourselves several weeks later.

The telephone call came on Friday morning, July 9, 1976. Paul was to have been married the next day.

Paul Lewis Young was born in Pittsburgh in 1893. He became my father-in-law in 1950. Paul never knew my father, who had died of cancer the year before. I wish they had met; both were missionaries and shared similar convictions and concerns.

Paul went to Ecuador in 1918 and was married there three years later. He and Alice Walker had two daughters. Alice died from tuberculosis at Christmastime, 1926.

Paul remarried in 1929. Berenice Carman Young died of cancer in 1970. There were no children from that marriage.

First serving with the Christian and Missionary Alliance, Paul later became the executive secretary of the United Bible Societies in Ecuador. Paul was one of the five pioneers of the missionary radio station HCJB in Quito.* He officially retired in 1963, but

---

*The book, *Come Up To This Mountain* (by Lois Neely, Tyndale House, 1980), tells the story of Clarence W. Jones, the pioneer missionary of radio station HCJB, and of the Ecuador Paul Young loved and where he worked. Paul is mentioned several times in the book.

that was a mere technicality; emotionally he never "let go."

Eventually, after Berenice's death, he rented an apartment in a retirement community near Kissimmee, Florida. He would spend a restless three or four months there, travel somewhere to visit or preach in the United States or Canada (sometimes to Puerto Rico or the Dominican Republic), and then find some excuse to return to Ecuador. We would normally learn about this ongoing international commuting by way of a hastily scribbled postcard mailed from Miami International Airport, probably minutes before his 2:00 A.M. flight to Quito was called.

On one of his trips to Ecuador he fell in love again and, at age eighty-three, planned to marry a missionary colleague, Evelyn Rychner. We learned the news by way of a letter, with photograph, only three weeks before the wedding date. Then we had a telephone call from Paul in Florida, telling of his safe arrival and saying that he soon would be leaving for Minnesota. He also urged us to attend the wedding (which we could not do).

The next word was that early-morning call from the doctor in St. Paul. There had been a wedding rehearsal, a dinner, and then the stroke.

Later, as I looked through Paul's many carefully annotated journals and diaries, I found this entry for July 8, 1976—the day he left Florida for Minnesota.

"Had blood pressure checked. 170/100 and was ordered back on Lassic."

It was the last entry he wrote with his right hand.

Still later, we found the medicine he should have taken in the trunk of his Dodge, which had been left in storage in Florida.

Throughout his life, Paul has been a Christian with singleness of vision and purpose. Younger missionaries were inspired by his insistent and persistent kind of personal evangelism. He constantly distributed tracts and Scripture portions. He led hundreds of people to a personal decision for Jesus Christ. He was never shy, never an introvert. He visited the president of Ecuador and gave him a Bible. In his so-called "retirement" years he held Penzotti Institutes in Chile, the Dominican Republic, Mexico, and Puerto Rico. (Francisco Penzotti was an Italian immigrant to Argentina who had a vision and plan of house-to-house distribution of the Scriptures throughout Latin America.)

Paul had few extracurricular activities, and even these were usually linked to his basic ministry of witnessing.

In his youth he had done harness racing and some boxing. His diaries indicate that he boxed a couple of times in Ecuador during the early 1920s, but only to make contact with a young man who was interested in boxing. Paul wanted to lead him to Christ. Paul considered sports a great waste of time and often said so, especially to his grandchildren.

He was extremely curious about nature and became an amateur botanist and zoologist. He collected animals for several U.S. zoos, in this way helping to put his daughters through Wheaton College. He met the famous Captain Allan Hancock and twice visited the Galapagos Islands with the captain and his crew on the *Valero II*.

Paul was a dowser. He possessed that mysterious sixth sense of being able to find water with a simple forked stick. Not all of his peers approved, and Paul would always bristle if someone called him—or any other dowser—a "water witch." He believed his special gift came from God. He discovered several good sources of water in Ecuador, and the wells are still pumping.

Paul enjoyed good health most of his life. He had problems with tropical fevers, but they had no lasting effect. His hearing was good. His eyesight was reasonably good. After his stroke, we learned that he had both a urological and a high blood pressure problem, but did not take the prescribed medication regularly. He was also careless about travel—going from sea level in Florida to eleven thousand feet in Quito, and back, without taking time for adequate "reentry."

He found it difficult to relax. It seemed he was compelled to be constantly doing "the Lord's work." Carolyn fondly remembers a couple of nature hikes with her father, but she cannot recall that her parents ever took a traditional family vacation.

Paul thought nothing of driving from Florida to Massachusetts over a long weekend. I learned after his stroke that he had had two potentially serious accidents, which affected his insurance rating. Paul carried no life nor health insurance (other than Medicare), believing, I suppose, that such provisions were unbecoming to a faithful Christian. He did not slow down, and no one helped him to slow down.

I think that somehow he expected to go on witnessing and working for his Lord until, like Enoch, he would simply enter the presence of his Master, who would continue to take care of him. The Lord did take care of Paul, through countless dangers and endeavors throughout his lifetime. But Paul did not take care of himself. His body finally rebelled; a blood vessel exploded, destroying part of the left side of his brain in what the doctors called a "massive" stroke.

Of course, the wedding was cancelled, and Evelyn and Paul had to work through their grief in their own ways. However, a greater tragedy for Paul continues. Throughout his life he has been a dedicated writer of journals; he was also a prolific correspondent. More importantly, to him, was his calling to be a personal worker, to witness to anyone and everyone he met, to verbalize the gospel. He wrote with his right hand, and his right hand is now paralyzed. He has not yet mastered writing with his left hand, although he can trace his name and a few letters.

Paul is an "expressive" aphasic—which means that his brain receives messages, but he cannot express his response in words, whether written or spoken. His speech is garbled and short-circuited. He is slowly learning the grace of being a Christian presence and is discovering a larger mission of intercessory prayer. But we know that his inability to speak and write is difficult and depressing for him.

Paul spent fifty-eight days in the St. Paul Ramsey Hospital. His stroke occurred in a city with one of the finest rehabilitative medical clinics anywhere, and it took only fifteen minutes to get him to this great university-related hospital. He received excellent therapy from the very outset—physical, occupational, and speech therapy—and he worked hard at his tasks, striving and pushing and hoping for the improvement that did not come.

Carolyn and I spent our vacation during August of 1976 looking at nursing homes in Texas and Florida. Paul's hospital bill was about five thousand dollars a month, and Medicare would pay most of this for only two months. We had to find an alternative that was practical and affordable, and it had to be found quickly.

We finally recommended that Paul return to central Florida, first for further evaluation by specialists at Florida Hospital in

Orlando and then, if the specialists concurred, that Paul take up residence in a nursing home facility adjacent to the retirement village where he had lived in Kissimmee, eighteen miles south of Orlando. We opted for Kissimmee because we felt this was the only place where Paul had tried to put down any roots, particularly after Berenice's death, and there likely would be friends there to provide a supportive group during his convalescence.

The specialists felt that Paul would benefit from some additional therapy, but that since his brain damage was extensive, dramatic improvement should not be expected. We were told that the prognosis for life expectancy following a stroke of this type was five years.

Esther and Carolyn closed Paul's apartment, placed his things in storage, and helped him get settled in the nursing home, where he had a semi-private room.

He remained in this nursing home for seven months. We made three visits from Texas during this period, and Esther made one from Maryland. It was a frustrating time for Paul, but it was equally frustrating for the rest of us, who were trying to monitor the situation by way of long-distance telephone.

We received no information from his doctor in Kissimmee. We received no reports from the nursing home; whenever we asked for information, we were made to feel that we were intruding. During this entire period I never once met or spoke with the administrator of the nursing home; I was always referred to a subordinate. Although there was a physical therapy room in the nursing home, it was never used for therapy.

On our first visit to Paul in Florida, we changed doctors. We learned there was a small rehabilitation clinic in the local community hospital. We arranged for Paul to get physical therapy and semi-weekly transportation to the hospital. Although we were grateful for the help he was now getting, we soon learned there was neither a resident occupational therapist nor a speech therapist in all of Osceola County. A speech therapist was available in Orlando, at an hourly charge of forty dollars plus mileage.

I don't want to berate that particular nursing home unduly. There were many good people there who tried to do their best. There were groups and individuals who tried to brighten lives with their visits. Several of them kept in touch with us. The therapist in Kissimmee went beyond her duty in helping Paul in extra ways.

However, the continuing support system we anticipated for Paul did not materialize. Three or four good "buddies" came by regularly; one came every day to shave Paul. But what we didn't realize then was that older people can't get about as easily nor as frequently as they would like to, that they have their own agendas and schedules, and that a few were simply uncomfortable being around handicapped people on a regular basis.

Carolyn, Andy (our youngest son), and I spent Christmas of 1976 with Paul. There was a community dinner involving more than thirty people; Paul's sister, herself nearly blind, came down from Orlando. It was a different kind of Christmas for us, but it was a happy time. Neverthless, we decided then that we would try to bring Paul to Austin.

This came about in April, 1977, and Paul lived in our home until March, 1979—almost two years.

We felt it was a good decision. Austin now had a rehabilitation clinic of its own (it didn't at the time of Paul's stroke). An excellent physiatrist (a medical doctor with special expertise in rehabilitative medicine) took charge and Paul began a steady regimen of three kinds of therapy. A graduate student at the University of Texas, working in audiology, did additional extensive work with Paul's speech problem.

After nine months of therapy, however, the specialist advised us to discontinue the program since Paul had reached a plateau and further improvement could not be anticipated.

Elsewhere I pay tribute to Juanita, the nurse's aide who made home care possible for us. But due to Juanita's illness and our inability to find a suitable replacement, Paul again entered a nursing home in 1979.

Carolyn, Paul, and I spent a month looking at varoius facilities in central Texas. This time we concentrated on church-related homes. The three of us finally agreed that Trinity Lutheran Home in Round Rock, fifteen miles north of Austin, was the best place we had seen.

No nursing home can be perfect, but after twelve months of observation we know that a special quality of Christian care exists in this home. The administrator's own mother lives there. The staff includes a resident chaplain and a physician, which is unusual for nursing homes. Of course, there is also a director of nursing, an activities director, and a competent staff aided by many volunteers. The nursing home is located on forty acres, and its lawns and live oaks resemble a park.

Paul isn't always happy with his situation, but he seems to have adapted well. He has been accepted by the other residents, who greet and respect him as "Pastor Young."

Paul still gives out tracts and encourages others to go with him to the daily chapel service, the weekly Bible class, and the Tuesday evening hymn sing. Thus, Paul has some continuing sense of active ministry.

He was never much of a reader, but now Paul listens to many tapes—the talking books available through the Library of Congress, the recorded versions of Scripture, and the cassette versions of the *Unshackled!* radio programs.

His television set has become a window to the world. He watches the news. He follows politics (we secured a voter registration card for him and he is able to vote by absentee ballot). He has become a fan of *Little House on the Prairie* and *The Waltons*. He enjoys any programs related to nature, such as the *National Geographic* specials and *Wild Kingdom*. The cable brings him programs from the Christian Broadcasting Network. And he even watches some sports now. He saw the 1980 Super Bowl—perhaps because his old home town of Pittsburgh was involved. And he enjoyed watching the Winter Olympics of 1980.

The chapter on transportation describes some of the places we've been able to visit together. I simply want to stress here that we've tried to widen Paul's world in ways beyond television. I took him to his first circus, and his eyes sparkled and his jaw dropped at the thrills and the color, just as though he were a little boy. We've taken him to see the Royal Lippizaner horse show and the Black Watch Scottish Guard.

We've even taken him to see a few movies (which may shock some of his friends!), and Paul enjoyed them. He has become a fan of Corrie ten Boom, and has seen *The Hiding Place*. He laughed at *All Things Bright and Beautiful*. He was stirred by *Born Again* and the Genesis Project production of *Jesus*. Loving horses as he does, Paul liked *The Black Stallion*. He has seen *Joni*; we'd read the book to him and Paul has seen her on the Billy Graham crusade specials.

He is beginning to enjoy using his left hand in creating color. He is using mostly paint-by-number books, but he has discovered that he can create something colorful and beautiful. He made posters one Christmas for his grandchildren.

I do believe that Paul is finally beginning to learn to relax and to rest in his Lord.

3

Anna Batutis Gillies

Ten years before Paul's stroke, we received a call from Chicago. It was the summer of 1966, and we were living in Elkhart, Indiana.

The call was from a friend, telling me there had been an accident and that my mother was in a hospital. The "accident" turned out to be a robbery; my mother had been struck on the right side of her head with a revolver. She was sixty-five at the time and planning to retire soon. She was working as a desk clerk and living at the Leland Hotel, a small hotel for women, located on Harrison Street on the south fringe of Chicago's Loop. My mother was struck because she talked back to the robber.

I believe her deterioration began with that blow. At any rate, today my mother is seriously disoriented due to severe brain damage.

Like Paul, Anna Batutis was also born near Pittsburgh. Her parents emigrated from Lithuania, and she married a Lithuanian immigrant. Her foundry-worker father died from respiratory complications before her first birthday. Her mother died before she was three. Thus, Anna grew up as a true orphan, cared for by an older alcoholic stepbrother who shifted her from boardinghouse to boardinghouse and who often dropped out of sight for months at a time. It must have been a terribly lonely and insecure existence for her. The stepbrother eventually committed suicide.

Anna survived because she was a maverick. She attended a Sunday school held in her public school by local United Presbyterians. She won a scholarship to Shauffler Institute in Cleveland and then to the Methodist Training Institute in Chicago. She received either a degree or a certificate in social work, and applied that training in her subsequent missionary and church outreach programs.

She married my father on New Year's Eve, 1924. Anton had just been graduated from the Northern Baptist Seminary, and he was almost twenty years older than she. I was born the following year, their only child. My father died in 1949; Anna has been a widow for more than three decades.

I had no grandparents, but life with my father was similar to life with a grandfather, as he was forty-four when I was born.

Their work took my parents to many cities with large Lithuanian communities, although Chicago remained their base. They went to Lithuania in 1937, as my father planned to establish the first Protestant orphanage in that country. But those plans and his work were shattered by World War II.

Later, my parents spent a term of missionary service in Argentina. My mother enjoyed working with children and youth, but as their work grew she became more of an office manager and bookkeeper, work for which she was not trained and which frustrated her. I believe her years in Lithuania were the happiest of her life.

Anna had many medical problems that have not persisted; she enjoys relative good physical health today. She had tuberculosis during her pregnancy and spent several months in a sanitorium after I was born. She had a hysterectomy in 1930—obviously a traumatic experience for a woman only twenty-nine years old. In later years, her thyroid and gall bladder were removed.

After my father died, Anna wandered and traveled. She sold the two-apartment house in Chicago, on which only a small mortgage remained. We argued about that because I thought the rental income would be needed. I still feel that one more uprooting in her life was not healthy.

Anna visited us in Texas several times, going on to Mexico to work with some of her friends in Monterrey. Despite her time in Argentina, her Spanish was hesitant. But she communicated easily with the children she loved. She traversed the United States, visiting old school friends and converts and "graduates" of the mission. Within three years her savings—including the proceeds from the sale of the house—were gone.

Once the wandering was out of Anna's system, she gladly returned to Chicago, which she really considered home. She worked as a switchboard operator in a large hospital for a while, but in those pre-automation days the pressure of that job was more than she could handle. She ultimately found a job as a desk clerk at the Leland Hotel. It didn't pay much, but she was able to rent a room at a reasonable price and she could observe the action and excitement of a huge metropolis, as Chicago's Loop was literally her front yard. But the robbery, which put her in the hospital, quickly altered her life.

When Anna retired, her Social Security income allowed her to live comfortably with three other ladies. They shared an apartment and a kitchen, but they did not share meals, and Anna did not eat as well as she could have or should have. I believe that poor nutrition contributed to her deterioration.

We had returned to the Midwest and were living in Indiana during the mid-sixties. We enjoyed her visits from Chicago. She seemed pleased to play the role of grandmother. She took over the household at least twice while Carolyn and I combined business trips with some vacation.

But there were signs that things were not going well. Anna repeated herself to an irritating degree. She seemed especially upset about the changing nature of her neighborhood in Chicago. Once she began to tell a story, it was like a record that had to play itself out to the end; every phrase was predictable.

I tried to see her as often as possible when I got into Chicago. It was best to see her in her apartment. More and more often, when we agreed to meet at Marshall Field's or some other downtown site, I was stood up. Anna was forgetting immediate details, and her universe was shrinking.

A new chapter began in 1974. The four ladies had to give up their apartment. One had a hip injury that required skilled nursing care. Two decided to settle in a retirement community. We decided that Anna should move with us, as we were returning to Texas.

She lived with us for about a year. We saw that she ate more nutritiously. We were able to monitor her appearance, both in terms of dress and hygiene. We were able to involve her in volunteer work three days a week in day-care centers. We saw how much she enjoyed playing with and touching the children. We took her to a Baptist church where she found new Sunday school friends.

Nevertheless, Anna was becoming more confused. She enjoyed walking but frequently got lost whenever she did more than walk around our block. She could not remember the room of her Sunday school class from week to week. Nor could she remember where the entrance was to the day-care center where she did her volunteer work. Each time we would drive her to the center she would ask in a pleading, bewildered way, "Where do I go? What do I do?"

One day she didn't wait for us to pick her up. Instead, she began walking in the wrong direction. We called everyone we could think of and eventually called the police and reported her missing. The police found her several hours later, fifteen miles from our home. She had walked at least nine of those fifteen miles, going southeast instead of north. Except for being very tired, Anna probably didn't realize what had happened. We were disturbed, but the day-care people were distressed. They hinted strongly that perhaps Anna's usefulness and reliability with young children may have come to an end.

Obviously, some kind of change had to be made. We could not afford a daytime sitter, and we did not know if Anna would accept a companion. I did not feel that she required nursing home care, even though Carolyn and I began to make visits and inquiries.

We discovered an alternative at just the right time.

A retirement residence called "The Governor's" had been established with funding from the Roman Catholic diocese of Austin (later we learned that most of the 120 residents were Baptists!). A former five-story dormitory near a university campus had been leased. Rooms were private with connecting baths. There was a lovely lounge area and an attractive dining room-cafeteria. A few residents showed some signs of confusion and senility, but all were ambulatory. The manager was a former chef and food services director, and "The Governor's" provided wholesome, tasty, and attractive food three times a day, with snacks in between. With Anna's small Social Security check and our contribution, it was affordable.

Since the residence was close to a university campus, there was lots of activity. Anna's room on the fifth floor had a good view of Guadalupe Street, with its traffic and people. Anna made friends, and together they would walk around the block, speaking to people, picking flowers (that probably shouldn't have been picked), and returning for a cup of coffee and a cookie. We visited her during the week and took her to her church on Sundays and to our home for Sunday dinner. We had a private telephone installed for her; I wanted her to have the security of calling me whenever she felt the need (she never did) and I wanted a way of keeping in immediate touch. The retirement residence seemed to be an ideal example of "congregate living," where older people supported and looked after each other.

The manager thought the situation would be more ideal if an experienced social worker could be employed to direct activities and to help individual residents successfully maintain their independent living. But he was unable to secure the funding from his board or from the Department of Public Welfare. In retrospect, this was ironic. While the residents were not yet welfare recipients, many of them would become recipients when they entered nursing homes. One wonders whether institutionalization might have been deferred had adequate social service counseling been available early enough.

Seven months after Anna took up residence in "The Governor's," it was decided to move the residence several blocks away. The board of directors purchased a former conference center. It was three stories high; there were many more meeting rooms; and bedrooms were clustered into suites of three, with a small lounge and two bathrooms. The new location was called "The Whitestone."

It was another unfortunate uprooting for Anna. Although the move was only a few blocks from the old residence, the location of her room and the landmarks of her neighborhood had all changed. No longer could she observe passing traffic from her room. She couldn't remember her room number and she constantly lost her key. The halls were long and tunnel-like.

Directors also changed. Food was still ample and good, and

the new director was as caring as the old, but continuity had been broken and Anna's life-style had been altered. Her support system remained more or less intact, since most of the residents moved with her. However, many of them were also confused and uncertain about the changes that had taken place. It was beyond their control and comprehension.

We saw new signs of deterioration in Anna. Once she had been an avid and intense reader; now she no longer read. She also began to miss her meals. Often I would find her barricaded in her room; she had pushed all the movable furniture against the door. Her insecurity was pathetic. She was constantly packing and unpacking suitcases. I thought the kindest thing to do was to remove the suitcases. She then packed and unpacked her dresser drawers, placing her things in neat piles around the room, on the floor, or on her bed. I can't remember how many times Carolyn and I replaced dresses on hangers and personal items in drawers.

We still tried to involve her in church and in our family celebrations. We began to make sure she got a good bath whenever she visited us. Only showers were available at "The Whitestone," and Anna didn't always use hers. Getting her in the mood for a bath became both a game and a challenge.

The problem of personal hygiene became more acute. I now think that Anna was reverting more and more to childhood insecurities and bathroom patterns. What follows isn't a pleasant description, but it must be written. Some of you may face something similar. It's traumatic for a child to face the earthy reality of a parent's deterioration.

Anna no longer used the toilet, which was just outside her door. Instead, she used whatever container she found within her room—perhaps a wastepaper basket but more often a cardboard carton she had found somewhere.

Carolyn and I tried to think of ways we could help her with this problem. I thought that since Anna turned off all the lights in her room, she simply couldn't find her way to the bathroom at night. So I put night lights into every socket. Anna promptly removed every one, and unplugged every lamp as well.

I made a sign for her door. She had to see it when the door

was closed. It said "BATHROOM" and was underlined with an arrow. But it wasn't observed. How could it be, in the dark?

Carolyn thought we ought to get an old-fashioned chamber pot—something Anna might have used in her childhood and boardinghouse days. They are not stocked in a typical department store, but we finally found one in a large hardware store. It's now stored in our garage; I don't think it was ever used.

My office was located just two blocks from "The Whitestone," and I was able to see Anna almost daily. Much of my visit was taken up with cleaning and airing out her room, helping her to look more presentable, and getting her into the dining room for some food.

I'll never forget one afternoon. My mother was resting, but awake—barricaded in her room. When she finally admitted me and I opened the shades, I saw the reason for the stench that permeated the room. Not only had she had a loose bowel movement, but she had not found a container. The excrement was scattered from her bed to the closet, all over the shag rug. I didn't report the condition to the management, since only weekly maid service was provided. But I was also too embarrassed then to make a report.

You do what you have to do. I got Anna up and washed her hands and backside. I have learned with both Paul and Anna that I must set aside inhibitions where hygiene is concerned. After Anna was cleaned up, I helped her to get dressed and escorted her to the lounge, hoping she would stay interested in the magazines I put before her. I went out to buy disinfectant, a scrub brush, and paper towels. The cleanup job took a couple of hours, and I don't think the management ever knew what had happened.

We now knew that Anna needed help that neither we nor the retirement home could provide. After extensive testing—including an EMI brain scan—the specialist told us that Anna had probably suffered a stroke. There was shrinkage of the "temporal lobe," the area for memory, and the ventricles of the brain had been enlarged. His prognosis: The abnormalities were not treatable.

This was background for the diagnosis of "senile dementia." I remember how the term first shocked me. It sounded too much like "demented," and that word conjured up images of mental institutions. Eventually I learned that "dementia" simply means "loss or impairment of mental powers due to organic causes."

Our family doctor finally laid down the law. He said that Anna could not remain where she was; she required skilled attention. Neither, he said, should we consider resumption of home care. Anna required specialized help and routine, and needed a sense of security, the kind available in a skilled nursing home. If we weren't ready to make the decision, he would.

I struggled with the decision for two months. Paul's stroke had since occurred and he was in the Florida nursing home. Carolyn and I already had misgivings and guilt feelings about that. Furthermore, I was working for the Texas Department of Human Resources, and one of my writing-production assignments was to work on "alternative care for the aging." In my research I had visited many nursing homes, interviewed many experts, and read many studies. I knew—or thought I knew—what would lie ahead for Anna.

The residents at "The Whitestone" didn't help, either. When they heard I was considering a nursing home for Anna, many of them turned on me with accusations and warnings. They didn't feel Anna was a problem. They would see that she got her meals; they would look after her. They meant well, yet I knew these good and generous people did not have the vaguest notion of Anna's mental condition. Neither did they know how terribly disturbed and frightened she was in her room, when she was away from the rest of them.

The decision was finally made in July of 1977 (Paul was now living with us). We chose a new facility in northwest Austin that had more than three hundred patients. Anna was admitted at the lowest level of required care.

In November, 1977, Anna fell and broke her hip. Falls are always feared by the elderly and are dangerous for them since their bones are brittle. She was taken to the hospital, where a hip joint was replaced. I'm sure that her ten days in the hospital were excruciatingly frightening for her. It seemed that her life now was one uprooting after another.

When she returned to the nursing home, she moved slowly with a walker and was in considerable pain. She was moved to a section of the nursing home where a higher level of care was given. The new room and new surroundings probably added to her disorientation. She walked much less and began to spend most of her time sitting in a chair next to the nurses' station. There would be ten to fifteen others beside her passing their hours in the same pathetic, apathetic way.

Anna took no interest in crafts or games or television. She had her own radio and TV set, but would not—or could not—operate either one. Eventually she was moved to a third unit, which provided the maximum level of care. There didn't seem to be enough staff and there was frequent turnover of personnel, but this situation is common to most nursing home facilities. Anna was simply marking time.

Meanwhile, a nursing home was built just five blocks from our home. Carolyn and I learned that it was licensed as a "skilled-care" facility (the highest level of care), was smaller (110 beds), and appeared to be less institutional. We thought it would be an improvement, particularly because we would be better able to monitor her care. So once again, poor Anna was moved.

It was a long walk from her new room to the dining room, and I purchased a wheelchair for her. This may have been a mistake, because she now spends most of her waking moments in that wheelchair. She stands with difficulty and pain, and it has been months since I have seen her take a single step.

Although she smiles much of the time, Anna is mostly withdrawn. She used to be an excellent vocalist, but she no longer sings. The right side of the brain controls the musical and symbolic part of our activity, and that revolver blow of many years ago hit her right temple and may have caused the injury. She reads no books, works no puzzles, and does not sew. She leafs disinterestedly through an occasional magazine, eats mostly with her fingers, and is totally incontinent. Her speech is gibberish. I doubt whether she knows I am her son. Carolyn is merely a friendly stranger and frequent visitor.

All we can do for Anna now is to check on the quality and nature of her care and be sure she is as comfortable as possible. Meanwhile, we must assure her that she is loved.

I'm visiting her more frequently at noontime. It gives me a chance to see the quality and kind of food being served (it is quite good). I try to remind her to use her fork and spoon, and often I feed her.

Carolyn keeps a close eye on Anna's clothes, repairing and replacing them when necessary. We provide disposable pads for Anna's comfort and for the staff's convenience. We keep her nails trimmed and clean. We've arranged to have her hair cut every six weeks. Occasionally we're able to go out together for a drive. More frequently, we simply push her in her wheelchair outdoors in the warm Texas sun—and when Texas is cold and rainy, we wander with her through the corridors. We attend vespers with her and try to keep her interested. We remember her anniversaries. We bring her little presents. We hold her hand, rub her back, kiss her, and tell her often that we love her. We pray that God's Spirit will surround her with His love and peace in a special, intuitive way.

It so happens that I am writing this chapter about Anna on her birthday. She is seventy-nine. My eyes are moist with the memories of the past and the wishes for something better and livelier.

But I know Anna will not improve.

4

Alternatives You Should Consider

Old age isn't so bad
When you consider the alternative.
—Maurice Chevalier (1888-1972)

Once upon a time, families did not move much. Wage-earners did not change jobs every two, three, or four years. Once upon a time, American families were mostly rural or lived in small towns. Their houses were big, could easily be enlarged, and the families were large. Once upon a time, mothers stayed at home. It was expected that father and mother, and grandfather and grandmother, would end their years in their own homes, which were probably only a few doors or blocks from the homes of their children, if not actually *in* their children's homes.

Once upon a time, before the era of dozens of technological inventions to make home care and cooking easier, faster, and more efficient, there were enough essential chores for every member of the family. The old folks were needed at home.

We saw some of this older tradition in the Amish communities in northern Indiana. But for most of us, this era has passed; it's now "once upon a time." Our homes and our families are smaller. It is no longer practical to take aging parents with us when we move, even if they wanted to come and even if we had the room.

The ideal situation for our parents is still the one where they can manage their lives without interference and intervention—a situation that enables them to live, to shop, to garden, to socialize, and to worship where and as they wish. There are ways we may be helpful in facilitating such independent living for them.

When totally independent living is no longer possible, several alternatives exist. Some of these will be looked at in greater detail in later chapters. However, in summarizing the alternatives here

I want to emphasize that the nursing home is by no means the *only* alternative to independent living.

Independent Living

Your aging parents may have a home or an apartment in which they may continue to live. If they own their own property and it isn't too large for them to handle, parents should be encouraged to hold on to such accommodations. They'll be happier and their living costs will be lower.

If one or both parents recently suffered an accident or some handicapping illness, it may be necessary to do some remodeling, particularly in kitchens and bathrooms. More specifics will be detailed in Chapter 5.

When parents continue to live independently, find ways to check on them and their situation without destroying their independence. If they are capable of independent living, they should be allowed to live it. However, you need to be sure of that capability. A regular visit will allow you to see if things are under control. Perhaps you could take responsibility for heavier chores—putting up storm windows, weatherstripping, or making certain repairs. If you live some distance away from your parents, arrange for a neighbor or a nearby friend to check on them by telephone and in person; it's helpful to have a third person's reaction and evaluation.

You can keep in frequent telephone contact yourself. Install a telephone if your parents don't have one or no longer feel they need one. Be sure it's conveniently placed—or arrange for an additional extension at bedside. The commercials are true—it *is* possible to reach out and keep in touch, to remind each other of love and concern by the warmth and personality of one's voice. You can discern much of the emotional and physical well-being of your parents by hearing them speak—or not speak.

The telephone is essential, of course, in emergencies. You might affix a list of emergency numbers to each telephone in your parents' home. Include the local doctor's number and your own telephone number (identify it so a stranger would know whom to call first).

Find out if there is a telephone reassurance program in the

city where your parents live. Such programs are often sponsored by civic groups or churches, and they provide your parents with a number they can call anytime to reach someone who will listen and help.

Retirement Centers

Retirement communities are becoming increasingly available and popular. They range from clusters of individual units to high-rise apartment-type dwellings. Sometimes older hotels or motels are remodeled for a new use. "The Governor's" and "The Whitestone," where Anna lived, were recycled residences that provided "congregate" or "sheltered" living.

Living space will always be reduced in such facilities, and parents usually must decide carefully which personal items they will retain. A few keepsakes and favorite pieces of furniture help to bridge the change from one's former home to the new residence, which in time ought to become a new *home*.

Some retirement centers provide a dining room where meals may be eaten in a cafeteria or restaurant setting. Sometimes only noon and evening meals are served, allowing the resident to prepare his or her own breakfast. Often a choice is available— one may eat with others in a dining room or prepare meals in one's own room or apartment.

Some centers are built next to convalescent facilities, but retirement communities are not nursing homes. They provide no medical assistance and are prohibited by law from doing so. Residents must usually be ambulatory and be able to care for themselves. A few centers provide what is called a "life care" guarantee—which includes future nursing care whenever needed—but such arrangements are costly.

Retirement centers have the advantages of pleasant surroundings without the need to keep up a yard. Security is provided around the clock. There is value in sharing a common, caring life within a community that offers stimulating activities and involvement for active older citizens.

Ask whether pets and gardens are allowed. These are important to many retirees. What restrictions are there, if any, for "normal" living?

Since costs and plans vary, retirement residences should be investigated carefully, perhaps with legal advice.

If federal funding helped build such a retirement facility, there is usually no down payment required. Monthly "rents" are pegged to one's income. Such housing may have been built by a municipality or a nonprofit organization or church.

Privately financed facilities always require some kind of down payment. Such entrance fees can be substantial, and high monthly "maintenance" assessments may also be required. Down payments may be nonrefundable or in the form of required purchase of bonds or annuities. Read the prospectus and contract carefully before signing it. Do the proceeds of the entrance fee revert to the sponsoring organization upon the resident's death, or do they became part of the resident's estate? What are the rights of the surviving spouse?

Don't make a decision merely on the basis of a printed brochure or prospectus, a telephone conversation, or even someone's recommendation. Visit the facility. Observe and evaluate it for yourself, with your parent if possible. Take your time when you visit. If it is permitted, have a meal there. Observe the ongoing activities and facilities for hobbies. How close are shopping centers and churches? Is the facility in the country or in the city? If possible, chat with residents and get their reactions. A future home is involved, so make this a joint decision with your parent.

Day Activities Centers

Many groups now sponsor day-care or day activities centers for older persons. These are held in churches, in storefront facilities, or in new specially designed neighborhood centers.

Supervised activities are held throughout the day—usually from eight until five.

Activities include games, crafts, "reality therapy" (I'll explain this term later), exercise, field trips, shopping sprees, special programs of slides and music, conversation, and a well-balanced hot noon meal (sometimes provided through a delivered-meal or "meals-on-wheels" program).

Transportation is sometimes provided by the center.

Participants must usually be ambulatory, be able to help and serve themselves, and manage restroom needs on their own.

In some areas where nursing home occupancy is down, nursing homes are cooperating with state social service agencies to develop day-care activities centers within nursing home facilities. Since some nursing or paramedical staff is available, wider participation—including that of handicapped persons—is possible. Great Britain has many "day hospitals" where patients return to their own homes at night. Use of nursing homes as day activities centers would be a similar approach.

The purpose of a day activity center is to provide a safe, secure, and exciting place for an older person to spend the day, whether he or she lives independently or in the home of a friend or relative.

Foster Care or Group Care

Because welfare agencies are seeking alternatives to more expensive nursing home care, increasing attention is being given to new models of group (or "sheltered") living that might provide supportive and safe care for the aging.

Just as some families take in children with special needs, foster homes for adults with special needs are also being sought. A couple or family who owns a large home might be able to provide shelter and food for three or four adults. One or both "foster helpers" may be eligible to receive compensation for their labor as well as for providing room and board. Necessary nursing care might be provided through a public health service or some other approved provider of home medical care.

A foster home may be preferable for those who require some medical and custodial care, but who do not require the twenty-four-hour skilled care that nursing homes are designed to provide—and for which charges must be higher. In many cases, a good foster home provides a happier and less structured environment than a nursing home or even a relative's home. Those in the group help one another.

Sometimes grouping or association is spontaneous. Three to five individuals might discover a compatibility and decide to rent a house or apartment together, sharing expenses and responsibilities. Women, particularly widows with limited resources, frequently combine funds and interests in some common arrangement. Today this is called "congregate living."

There is nothing new about sharing a large house or apartment with others; boardinghouses and tourist homes were precursors of this idea. What is new is the possibility of securing reimbursement from state agencies for "chore care" or "homemaker" services. Social service agencies are seeking innovative ways to extend the value of inflated dollars, while keeping persons not requiring skilled care out of nursing homes.

Most welfare agencies have an administrative unit dealing with the "aged, blind, and disabled" (sometimes called ABD programs). Persons from this unit can provide you with information about day activities centers and group-care facilities in your area.

Nursing Homes

Chapter 6 will discuss nursing homes in greater detail—particularly the criteria for choosing one. For now, let's just say that there *is* a place for nursing homes in the spectrum of care for the aging. These homes provide necessary services.

A nursing home does not have to be a way station on the road to the cemetery. Far too many elderly people (and their children) have this image of nursing homes and balk at even considering them.

Many states now require nursing homes to devise a release plan—which may include a rehabilitation (or resident-care) program—for every resident upon admission. I'm not yet convinced that most nursing homes do this with any great commitment, but it is a worthy goal. Many older patients who merely require convalescence should not be forced to pay the high cost of hospital care. Use of hospital beds should be limited to emergencies, to serious illnesses requiring specialized equipment and facilities, or to intensive postoperative care. Nursing homes can and do provide intermediate and short-term care; they used to be called "convalescent homes."

There may be times when an older person receiving health care in your home should become a temporary resident in a nursing home. You and your family may face an emergency that requires this, or you may simply need a vacation without the stress and strain of providing constant health care.

Nursing homes also provide long-term care. A person who requires around-the-clock medication, who needs an ongoing therapy program, or who is incontinent or generally disoriented may well require the special, skilled care that only a good nursing home can provide. If it is required, and especially if it is advised by your physician, explore the possibilities of nursing homes without feeling guilty or morbid.

Hospices

The dictionary defines *hospice* as "a place of shelter for travelers." The Latin word means "hospitality" (and isn't it intriguing that the word *hospital* is derived from *hospitality*!). In medieval times such way stations were usually maintained by monastic orders.

When Dr. Cicely Saunders opened St. Christopher's Hospice in London, England, in 1967, a new approach to care for the terminally ill was begun.

There may be as many as five hundred hospices in the United States. Their growth is limited by finances, the need for state approval and licensing, and massive opposition by segments of the commercial nursing home industry.

Hospices provide support services to families who keep terminally ill loved ones in their homes. They also provide institutional care facilities—small, pleasant, hospital-type structures, usually with less than fifty beds. Hospices exist to care for those who have been diagnosed as having a terminal disease (usually cancer) for which the life expectancy is usually six months or less.

Hospices treat symptoms, not diseases. Medication is given for pain. Care is provided by physicians, nurses, social workers, pastors or pastoral counselors, psychiatrists, therapists, pharmacologists, family members, and volunteers in a holistic manner. Support is given not only to the patient, but also to the patient's family.

A few physicians have felt a special call to this new kind of ministry. It is *new* because in so many ways the hospice approach goes against a background and an education of physicians that has as its only objective helping people to get well.

The hospice movement helps patients and families face death with dignity and security, surrounding them with loving care and concern. Elisabeth Kübler-Ross makes special mention of the hospice environment in her book *To Live Until We Say Good-Bye* (Englewood Cliffs, N.J.: Prentice-Hall, 1978).

Sandol Stoddard, in his book *The Hospice Movement* (Briarcliff Manor, N.Y.: Stein and Day, 1977) provides this description:

People in hospices are not attached to machines, nor are they manipulated by drips or tubes, or by the administration of drugs that cloud the mind without relieving pain. Instead, they are given comfort by methods sometimes rather sophisticated but often amazingly simple and obvious, and they are helped to live fully in an atmosphere of loving kindness and grace until the time has come for them to die a natural death. It is a basic difference in attitude about the meaning and value of human life, and about the significance of death itself which we see at work in the place called *hospice*.

This newest alternative in caring for loved ones who are dying, and who know they are dying, is one many families may want to consider. The atmosphere in hospices is one of joy and celebration and hope. Surely this is an atmosphere with which Christians, especially, can identify.

Resources—Chapter 4

● Your state health department should have information about hospices in your area.

Anderson, Margaret. *Looking Ahead*. St. Louis: Concordia, 1978.
Dickinson, Peter A. *The Complete Retirement Planning Book*. New York: E. P. Dutton, 1976.
Musson, Noverre. *The National Directory of Retirement Residences*. New York: Frederick Fell Publishers, 1973.

5

A Special Look at Home Care

'Mid pleasures and palaces though we may roam,
Be it ever so. humble, there's no place like home;
A charm from the skies seems to hallow us there,
Which sought through the world is ne'er met with elsewhere.
—John Howard Payne (1791-1852)

Health care of your loved one—whether in your own home or in another—requires planning, patience, and modification of both your home and your life-style.

Sometimes the planning enters into your selection of a new home. When Carolyn and I returned to live in Austin, we had already decided that we would provide a place in our home for Anna.

"Independent" Living

Although Anna was showing increasing signs of disorientation, she was able to walk and care for most of her needs. We felt she needed some independence but that she also needed family close by. Thus, in our house-hunting Carolyn and I looked at single-family dwellings that offered a "mother-in-law" design—a bedroom with bath at the end of the house opposite where the rest of the family would be living.

What we found were homes either prohibitive in cost or impractical in design. Most "mother-in-law" arrangements were built adjacent to the kitchen or dining/living area. We felt that such proximity would inhibit what little entertaining we did, as well as the more boisterous habits of our teen-age son.

We finally purchased a four-bedroom home, with all four bedrooms located in the same general area. We assigned the master bedroom to Anna because it had its own bath.

The room seemed to be ideal for her. It had a large picture

49

window with a good view of our back yard and the garden. The room was large, allowing Anna plenty of room to spread out her things. She had already begun to empty dresser drawers periodically, laying out her garments as though preparing to pack her bags. Also, Anna was a scavenger and a scrapbook maker, cutting out figures and sketches and old Christmas cards. She needed lots of room.

Since Anna preferred to get up later than the rest of the family, we made provision for her to make breakfast in her own room, if she chose. We purchased a three cubic-foot refrigerator and stocked it with milk and juices and fruit. We bought a hot pot for her to boil water or heat soup. We did not install a hot plate, believing this would be less safe. We wanted Anna to be able to boil water for coffee or tea, to enjoy fruit whenever she wanted to, and to have milk for her breakfast cereals. We expected her to take her other two meals with the rest of the family.

It wasn't a bad arrangement for as long as it lasted. I think the criteria we established are valid for families able to afford a house with this much room, allowing for some independent living—as much or as little as the loved one is able to handle—without exclusion from the family. The trick, I guess, is to balance independence with realistic dependence.

I've already described some of Anna's deterioration. She began to wander off and get lost. She rarely ate breakfast. She became careless about her personal hygiene. She was confused about her work with children at the day-care center. It became evident that she was no longer able to cope with this level of independent living. The next stage for her would be the retirement center.

Modify or Remodel?

We learned a great deal from having Anna in our home, and we made new plans before Paul arrived.

First, Carolyn and I moved into the master bedroom. Paul would use the smaller bedroom we had used for eight months. (Frankly, we enjoyed having our own bathroom, the view of our yard, and *two* closets.)

During his seven months in the nursing home, Paul had lived in a semi-private room. Now he would have a room to himself again. Since he was a hemiplegic (paralyzed on his right side) and could walk only with assistance, we guessed he would have difficulty maneuvering his wheelchair through our relatively narrow hallway and over our wall-to-wall shag carpet. Thus, we had to plan some modification that would not totally alter our house nor upset the family and its routine.

Andy, our youngest son, was completing his senior year of high school. For several months, he and Paul would have to share the same bathroom. That would require special planning and patience on Andy's part.

My first step was to build ramps at the front entrance and the patio entrance. I made the ramps of half-inch exterior-grade plywood and one-by-six boards. I measured the height of the step but simply guessed at the degree of slope that seemed practical. I cut the boards into three identical triangles and nailed the plywood to these. I added a brace across the base of the back, using one-by-two stock, and notched the boards so the unit would fit flush against the house. (Obviously, the ramp had to be flush with the threshold.)

The ramps are sturdy but not heavy. They can be moved easily for sweeping and cleanup underneath. I painted them to match the brown stain of the house. The ramps are still there, even though Paul now lives in a nursing home. (He still comes to visit.) They show little wear after several years of rather intensive use. I'm so used to them myself that I think I would miss them.

The carpet gave us more trouble. We tried a long plastic runner in the hallway, but soon gave up on that idea. The plastic never stayed flat, and we didn't like the odor. A heavy woven runner might have done the trick, but we never tried one. We finally decided that since we were not about to rip out our carpet, Paul would simply have to get used to the shag. We would push his wheelchair and assist him with his walker as he made his way to his favorite chairs. He was able to maneuver his wheelchair alone outdoors on the concrete patio.

If you live in a two-story house, you might want to set aside a room at ground level for your parent's use. If this isn't practical, and if your parent cannot negotiate stairs, consider the lease or purchase of a stair elevator. Some models cost less than two thousand dollars and can be installed within several hours, with no structural change or additional wiring required in your house.

You also might want to make some provision for easier communication within the house. Wireless intercom units can be purchased in radio supply stores. You simply plug in as many stations or listening posts as you require.

We decided we didn't need this much modern technology for our particular needs. I purchased an ordinary bicycle bell and mounted it on Paul's wheelchair; he rang it when he needed to get our attention. There was a bicycle squeeze-type horn beside his bed to be used in an emergency. He didn't use it, but it was so loud it would have awakened the neighborhood.

If your parent is able to use a telephone, consider installing an extension in your parent's room. Twenty-five-foot telephone extension cords are inexpensive and are available in most hardware stores. A person with many local friends might need a personal telephone line.

Special Furniture and Fixtures

Next, we had to secure a hospital-type bed. This is what Paul had become accustomed to during his two months in the hospital and his seven months in the nursing home. We first rented a bed from a medical supply house. Paul's doctor authorized the rental, and Medicare paid some of the cost. Eventually we purchased a bed.

Why a *hospital* bed for someone who is disabled? This kind of bed is heavy duty, has firm springs, and has a water-repellent mattress. It includes hand cranks that lower or raise the head or the foot of the bed (more expensive models do this electrically). All these are comfort features for the person. The beds may also be ordered with bed rails on both sides; these add to the parent's security and to the caretaker's peace of mind. Eventually we decided the railings weren't necessary, and Paul was pleased when they were removed.

We also rented a "trapeze," a triangular device that is usually suspended over and clamped to the bed, and assists the person in pulling himself upright. Trapezes are also available with a floor stand and can be used with a chair or a bedside commode.

In the past, Paul had used a trapeze suspended over his bed, but since it was used only occasionally we decided later that it too was not needed.

Consideration also had to be given to toilet and hygiene needs. We purchased an adjustable-height, self-standing commode for Paul's bedroom, primarily for emergency needs. It had a regular toilet seat and cover, below which was a plastic pail that could be removed easily.

In the bathroom itself I installed railing around the commode, attached to the toilet seat bolts. These sidearm railings are a helpful aid to sitting and rising.

The average commode is only fifteen inches high, which is really too low for handicapped or arthritic persons. An elevated adjustable toilet seat that fits inside your present commode can increase the seat height up to six inches. Several types are available through medical supply stores. We removed the elevated unit whenever we had guests, but left the safety rails.

I installed a grab bar directly in front of the commode, mounted vertically. Paul could easily reach out and pull himself up to a standing position; later he learned how to pivot his body while holding onto this bar, as we prepared for his shower.

We were unable to give Paul a bath; none of us—neither Carolyn nor Juanita nor I—could manage to lift a 185-pounder in and out of a tub. Special plastic chairs, operated by hydraulic water pressure, allow you to raise or lower your parent into a bathtub. But these are expensive (around four hundred dollars), and we felt our bathroom wasn't large enough for one.

So we settled on giving Paul showers. I bought a stool that could be placed inside the bathtub, and replaced the shower head with a portable one connected to a plastic hose. This is ideal for shampooing as well as for bathing (remember that your parent may not be able to stand or can stand only briefly and with considerable difficulty).

Most important of all was a sturdy grab bar within the bathtub itself. I found one that could be installed the entire length of the tub without drilling. It had no suction cups, but the stainless steel bar was engineered so it could be tightened. The unit I purchased is called a "Lombard handrail" and is manufactured by a Detroit company. It's guaranteed not to break or crack tile and will support six hundred pounds. Several similar devices are available. Such grab bars are helpful not only for paralytics, but also for people with arthritis or back and heart problems.

A grab bar like the one in front of the commode was installed next to Paul's bed. He used this to pull himself up out of bed (which is why he stopped using the trapeze).

These grab bars must be sturdy and must be affixed to the studs inside your wall. Heavy-duty towel bars will not do. The kind we installed had quarter-inch-thick lug screws, which will not pull out of the stud. You may want to have a professional carpenter do the job. I invested in a stud-finder and did the job myself.

I purchased the grab bars—along with the commode riser and side rails—in a local medical supply store. You'll find these listed in telephone classified sections under "medical equipment and supplies" or "hospital equipment and supplies."

Another excellent source for such items is the Sears *Home Health Care Catalog.* We purchased the hospital bed, the portable commode, and two wheelchairs through Sears.

I recently discovered another source for sturdy grab bars that may be just a bit less expensive than the kind you get in medical supply stores. Check your local auto supply store that carries hardware for recreational vehicles. Heavy-duty grab handles for mounting outside trailer or van doors would do quite well in the home when mounted with lug screws into the studs.

These kinds of modifications cost money, but expenses can be kept lower if you are able to do all or some of the work yourself. I estimate that the ramps, the grab bars, the bath handrail, and the portable commode and additional commode units cost approximately three hundred dollars.

Help Through Therapy

It isn't enough just to install equipment. Your parent must learn to use such facilities properly and safely. Help is available in teaching your "patient" to manage more efficiently.

Because of Paul's disability we became acquainted with three kinds of therapists—physical, speech, and occupational.

The occupational therapist can help people adjust to home

care in new ways. He can help most handicapped people learn to brush their teeth or clean their dentures, shave, bathe, use the commode, dress, pull up their socks, feed themselves, and even do some minor cooking. Paul learned to button his shirt and to operate a zipper with one hand. There are many ingenious tools to help the handicapped—devices for reaching or picking up things or for pulling up socks, food bumpers that clamp to plates, easy-grip eating utensils, one-hand jar openers, oversize key holders, and devices to safely turn gas on or off.

Discuss your hopes and plans for home care with the occupational therapist. He or she may have important suggestions or modifications for your plans, as well as knowledge (and catalogs) of suppliers.

Furthermore, once you have decided upon basic modifications and installations, the occupational therapist can work with your parent to establish new habits so that the disability can be adapted to new surroundings.

For example, many of the newest therapy rooms have two types of bathrooms, designed for those who are limited to use of either their right or left hand. Learning the best way to get out of bed is also important to someone who is partially paralyzed. Occupational therapists like to know the floor plan of your home, and they welcome your participation. They want the disabled person to succeed in his new surroundings. Such therapy is available through most hospitals or special clinics; the therapists also work with patients in the home.

Mobility With Wheelchairs

I rented a wheelchair for Paul before purchasing one. Then I bought a wheelchair for Anna. You may be as surprised as I was at the variety of wheelchairs available. They range in price and style from "Hondas" to "Cadillacs."

Secure professional advice as to the best type of wheelchair for your loved one. A physical therapist can help. A physiatrist may prescribe a specific kind of wheelchair (and walker) for a disabled or handicapped person. When medically prescribed, insurance coverage may apply. The cost is also deductible for federal income tax purposes.

Wheelchairs can be as light as thirty-five pounds or as heavy as one hundred pounds (for a motorized unit). An average weight for a reasonably sturdy unit is about fifty-five pounds. Weight is important if you plan frequent transfer of your patient from wheelchair to car and back. Lifting a folded wheelchair in and out of a car can become a back-breaking activity.

If your parent cannot walk or walks very little and will be using a wheelchair throughout most of the day, purchase the sturdiest unit you can. Wheelchairs travel many miles. In Anna's nursing home a speed limit sign was posted in one hallway: "Walkers, 5 mph—Wheelers, 10 mph."

Wheelchairs should be sturdy because axles break and bearings wear out. In the past thirty months, Anna's chair has been in the repair shop twice for new bearings. Just in passing, if I buy another wheelchair for Anna it will likely be a non-portable "wheel-about" chair. This type of chair is sturdy—it has heavy-duty five-inch casters—and is half the cost of a wheelchair. Since Anna can only propel her wheelchair with her feet, this kind of chair is probably the most appropriate for her now.

Another kind of "wheel-about" chair is designed specifically for transporting people directly into showers. These are waterproof and rustproof and are only practical for use in a shower stall with no outer ledge.

Look for certain things when buying a wheelchair:

Is the plastic sturdy and washable?

Are the plastic covers affixed with screws and easily replaceable?

Are the footrests the swing-away type? Can they be removed? (This is often helpful in transferral to cars or bathtubs.)

Are the brakes adjustable and sturdy?

The footrests should be adjustable in height. Some footrests can be ordered with heel stops.

There are also seat belts designed for wheelchairs.

There are two kinds of armrests: full-size and half-size, or "desk-type." The latter usually is preferable, as it allows a person to get closer to a table or desk. Armrests that are adjustable in height and that are removable allow a person to more easily slide from chair to bed, for example.

Wheelchairs can be customized, particularly for heavier individuals. Seats come in widths of eighteen, twenty, twenty-two, or twenty-four inches.

Specialized wheelchairs are available with higher backs, which can be lowered to a reclining position. Others are designed for amputees; they feature a longer wheelbase for safer balance.

Motorized wheelchairs are battery-operated; the battery must be recharged daily. A simple fingertip control guides the unit forward, backward, or turns the chair sideways. The motorized wheelchair is heavy and not easily transported, but most are approved for transporting on aircraft, should this be necessary.

A motorized scooter is also available (brand name: *Brewer Portascoot*). The manufacturer says it is adaptable for 80 percent of handicapped persons. It cannot be used by quadriplegics, who require chest support in order to remain seated upright. The scooter is only twenty-three inches wide, is easily disassembled for transport, can be controlled with either hand, and has a swivel seat that can be raised or lowered. This type of vehicle lends itself to many factory and office situations where handicapped persons are employed.

Prices range from about three hundred dollars for standard wheelchairs purchased through mail-order houses to six hundred dollars or more through durable medical goods retail stores. Motorized wheelchairs can cost as much as two thousand dollars. The motorized scooter sells for under one thousand dollars.

If your parent spends a great deal of time in a wheelchair, you might want to buy some kind of cushion for greater comfort and to prevent friction sores. Cushions range from an inexpensive inflatable or foam rubber type to a much more costly plastic-gel-filled cushion (often used by truck drivers).

More on Furniture

The furniture in your home that will be used by a handicapped person should be sturdy. Remember that the disabled often rely on chair arms or table tops for leverage as they rise or sit down.

Solid armchairs and solid-top tables are preferable. Armless high-backed chairs and drop-leaf tables should probably be avoided. Rockers are risky, even with arms; if one must be used, you can learn to place one foot on one of the rocker arches to steady the chair as you assist a handicapped person to sit.

Tables and desks are normally thirty inches high, and most wheelchairs maneuver easily under these. However, drawers or panels can bruise knees. In such cases, you might want to raise the table by placing wooden blocks under each leg of the desk or table. I drilled a one-inch-wide hole a half-inch deep into each block and placed a leg into each hole. This makes a table or desk much less wobbly.

Sturdy folding tables can be moved anywhere, indoors or out, and are good surfaces for looking at large-print books or large picture books, making handicrafts, or various other activities.

Reducing Your Parent's Universe

Up to this point, we've been thinking primarily about rearranging *your* home for the care of your parent. However, the suggestions for safety and comfort apply wherever your parent is able to continue independent living.

If your parent or parents live alone, you may want to consider some additional modifications.

You could redesign shelves and storage space, putting everything at a lower, safer level. Older people who are not sure-footed shouldn't be climbing ladders or chairs, and many have difficulty reaching for things. Some occupational therapists recommend that kitchen islands be designed to allow a minimum of movement from storage to preparation to partaking of food. The experts also say that "smaller is better," especially in bathrooms. Many older people need walls or solid furniture or fixtures to hold onto in order to maintain balance. Keep this in mind as you rearrange furniture.

Have confidence in your own creative imagination as you plan to meet the specific needs of your aging or handicapped parents. Do a bit of role playing. In trying to decide what would be helpful in Paul's bathroom and bedroom, I imagined I was paralyzed in the way he is. You might want to borrow a wheelchair and literally wheel yourself through your house, just to see what it's like to traverse the rugs and halls or to negotiate thirty-inch-wide doorways.

Security in Your Parent's Home

Many older people are fearful of being harrassed or robbed. There are ways you can provide them with greater security and reassurance.

Install deadbolt locks on front and back doors. These aren't burglar-proof, but neither can they be easily jimmied. A chain lock at the front door allows the door to be partially opened for deliveries, but still provides some security. A tiny viewing device can provide a wide-angle, fish-eye view of whoever is outside the door.

Special locks are also available for windows and patio doors. Walk through the lock section of your hardware store to see what is available and applicable to your parent's home.

Consider a smoke alarm, and be sure your parent understands what to do if it is activated. Some of the more sophisticated TV cable systems offer fire and security monitoring on specially assigned channels. Telephone companies are experimenting with similar light-activated sensor services.

An automatic telephone dialing device might be helpful for your parent. One of the least expensive units provides up to twenty channels for preset calls. Your parent would only have to push a button marked *Fire, Police, Doctor,* or *(Your Name)*, and the call would go through without dialing. Some units provide a "recall key"; if the previous call was busy and did not go through, the unit remembers that number, and it will be redialed automatically when you press the "recall" button. This type of unit costs about $150.

Expect the Unexpected

When you decide to provide health care in your home, accept the reality that there will be accidents. They will probably be minor, but older people still fall and break bones. You can be cautious and take preventive measures, but realize that there are risks in homes *or* institutions.

Your parent may not be able to make it to the bathroom in time—or get your attention in time. Be prepared to deal with damp and sometimes stained rugs. Provide protection to chairs with prized upholstery. Keep a good disinfectant handy for cleaning wheelchairs regularly.

Expect nicks and scratches on furniture, because wheelchairs will be backed into them. Walls and door frames will show wear and tear. Expect to use furniture polish, spackling compound, furniture putty, and eventually plaster and paint. You might want to install metal or wooden protectors for well-trafficked exposed corners.

If we are to provide a loving and caring environment for *people,* we will have to risk some loss and damage to *things.*

Resources—Chapter 5

● Your physician may have a collection of *The Medical Clinics of North America* (published bimonthly by W. B. Saunders Co., Philadelphia). The May, 1969 edition (Vol. 53, No. 3), deals with *rehabilitation* and includes articles on helping the cancer patient, diagnosis of speech disorders in brain-damaged adults, telephone services for the disabled, driver education for the disabled, and a helpful chapter on home planning for the severely disabled.

● Pick up a *Home Health Care* catalog from your Sears store. Locate *durable medical goods* stores in the yellow pages of your telephone book.

● *The Whitaker Company* (41 Douglas Avenue, Yonkers, NY 10703) can provide you with information about stairway elevators, bath lifts, motorized scooters, and other patient aids.

● The *Portascoot* is manufactured by E. F. Brewer Co. (P.O. Box 159, Menomonee Falls, WI 53051).

● Durable medical goods stores can provide you with information about *Burke chairs.* These are available in various models of easy chairs, loungers, and even a commode. All have a built-in air chamber system (110 volts) that elevates the seat at an angle to assist handicapped persons in and out of the chair.

● Your local *American Red Cross chapter* offers courses in home health care, as well as in emergency procedures in first aid and CPR (cardiopulmonary resuscitation). All are worth taking.

● Check with *mental health/mental retardation* organizations about outreach programs that provide therapy in your home. Also consult the *public health service* about visiting nurse programs.

cilities. If he treats elderly people, then he visits nursing homes with some regularity. If you ask for recommendations, your doctor will level with you. Physicians know where quality care exists.

Check your telephone directory for additional leads. Ask your pastor about church-owned facilities in your area; many denominations are committed to this kind of ministry.

You can do some preliminary screening by telephone. Your doctor has told you what level of care is required. Ask if the facility provides this and whether there are vacancies.

Once you have narrowed your list, you might want to check with the Better Business Bureau to determine whether all are reputable facilities.

Then it is up to you to investigate the nursing homes for yourself. Take your time to observe and ask questions. Don't be rushed into making a decision.

A Check List

The following check list was prepared by HEW, now reorganized as the Department of Health and Human Resources (HHR). The list will help you to ask some of the right questions when you visit a nursing home.

	Yes	No
1. Does the home have a current license from the state?	____	____
2. Does the administrator have a current license from the state?	____	____
3. If you need and are eligible for financial assistance, is the home certified to participate in government or other programs that provide it?	____	____
4. Does the home provide special services such as a specific diet or therapy which the patient needs?	____	____
5. Location:		
a) Pleasing to the patient?	____	____
b) Convenient for patient's personal doctor?	____	____
c) Convenient for frequent visitors?	____	____

	Yes	No
d) Near a hospital?	——	——
6. Accident prevention:		
a) Well-lighted inside?	——	——
b) Free of hazards underfoot?	——	——
c) Chairs sturdy and not easily tipped?	——	——
d) Warning signs posted around freshly waxed floors?	——	——
e) Handrails in hallways and grab bars in bathrooms?	——	——
7. Fire safety:		
a) Meets federal and state codes?	——	——
b) Exits clearly marked and unobstructed?	——	——
c) Written emergency evacuation plan?	——	——
d) Frequent fire drills?	——	——
e) Exit doors not locked on the inside?	——	——
f) Stairways enclosed and doors to stairways kept closed?	——	——
8. Bedrooms:		
a) Open into hall?	——	——
b) Window?	——	——
c) No more than four beds per room?	——	——
d) Easy access to each bed?	——	——
e) Drapery for each bed?	——	——
f) Nurse call bell by each bed?	——	——
g) Fresh drinking water at each bed?	——	——
h) At least one comfortable chair for each patient?	——	——
i) Reading lights?	——	——
j) Clothes closet and drawers?	——	——
k) Room for a wheelchair to maneuver?	——	——
l) Care in selecting roommates?	——	——
9. Cleanliness:		
a) Generally clean, even though it may have a lived-in look?	——	——
b) Free of unpleasant odors?	——	——
c) Incontinent patients given prompt attention?	——	——

	Yes	No
10. Lobby:		
a) Is the atmosphere welcoming?		
b) If also a lounge, is it being used by residents?		
c) Furniture attractive and comfortable?		
d) Plants and flowers?		
e) Certificates and licenses on display?		
11. Hallways:		
a) Large enough for two wheelchairs to pass with ease?		
b) Hand-grip railings on the sides?		
12. Dining room:		
a) Attractive and inviting?		
b) Comfortable chairs and tables?		
c) Easy to move around in?		
d) Tables convenient for those in wheelchairs?		
e) Food tasty and attractively served?		
f) Meals match posted menu?		
g) Those needing help receiving it?		
13. Kitchen:		
a) Food preparation, dishwashing, and garbage areas separated?		
b) Food needing refrigeration not standing on counters?		
c) Kitchen help observe sanitation rules?		
14. Activity rooms:		
a) Rooms available for patients' activities?		
b) Equipment (such as games, easels, yarn, kiln) available?		
c) Patients using equipment?		
15. Special-purpose rooms:		
a) Rooms set aside for physical examinations or therapy?		
b) Rooms being used for stated purpose?		
16. Isolation room:		
a) At least one bed and bathroom available for patients with contagious illness?		

	Yes	No

17. Toilet facilities:
   a) Convenient to bedrooms? ___ ___
   b) Easy for a wheelchair patient to use? ___ ___
   c) Sink? ___ ___
   d) Nurse call bell? ___ ___
   e) Hand grips on or near toilets? ___ ___
   f) Bathtubs and showers with nonslip surfaces? ___ ___
18. Grounds:
   a) Residents can get fresh air? ___ ___
   b) Ramps to help handicapped? ___ ___
19. Medical:
   a) Physician available in emergency? ___ ___
   b) Private physician allowed? ___ ___
   c) Regular medical attention assured? ___ ___
   d) Thorough physical immediately before or upon admission? ___ ___
   e) Medical records and plan of care kept? ___ ___
   f) Patient involved in developing plans for treatment? ___ ___
   g) Other medical services (dentists, optometrists, etc.) available regularly? ___ ___
   h) Freedom to purchase medicines outside home? ___ ___
20. Hospitalization:
   a) Arrangement with nearby hospital for transfer when necessary? ___ ___
21. Nursing services:
   a) R.N. responsible for nursing staff in a skilled nursing home? ___ ___
   b) L.P.N. on duty day and night in a skilled nursing home? ___ ___
   c) Trained nurses' aides and orderlies on duty in homes providing some nursing care? ___ ___
22. Rehabilitation:
   a) Specialists in various therapies available when needed? ___ ___

	Yes	No
23. Activities program:		
a) Individual patient preferences observed?	___	___
b) Group and individual activities?	___	___
c) Residents encouraged but not forced to participate?	___	___
d) Outside trips for those who can go?	___	___
e) Volunteers from the community work with the patients?	___	___
24. Religious observances:		
a) Arrangements made for patient to worship as he pleases?	___	___
b) Religious observances a matter of choice?	___	___
25. Social services:		
a) Social worker available to help residents and families?	___	___
26. Food:		
a) Dietitian plans menus for patients on special diets?	___	___
b) Variety from meal to meal?	___	___
c) Meals served at normal times?	___	___
d) Plenty of time for each meal?	___	___
e) Snacks?	___	___
f) Food delivered to patients' rooms?	___	___
g) Help with eating given when needed?	___	___
27. Grooming:		
a) Barbers and beauticians available for men and women?	___	___
28. General atmosphere friendly and supportive?	___	___
29. Residents retain human rights?		
a) May participate in planning treatment?	___	___
b) Medical records kept confidential?	___	___
c) Can veto experimental research?	___	___
d) Have freedom and privacy to attend to personal needs?	___	___
e) Married couples may share room?	___	___

	Yes	No
f) All have opportunities to socialize?	____	____
g) May manage own finances if capable, or obtain accounting if not?	____	____
h) May decorate own bedrooms?	____	____
i) May wear own clothes?	____	____
j) May communicate with anyone without censorship?	____	____
k) Are not transferred or discharged arbitrarily?	____	____
30. Administrator and staff available to discuss problems?		
a) Patients and relatives can discuss complaints without fear of reprisal?	____	____
b) Staff responds to calls quickly and courteously?	____	____
31. Residents appear alert unless very ill?	____	____
32. Visiting hours accommodate residents and relatives?	____	____
33. Civil rights regulations observed?	____	____
34. Visitors and volunteers pleased with home?	____	____

Caveat Emptor—"Let the Buyer Beware"

Here are additional questions to consider.

Is the facility both Medicare and Medicaid approved? Medicare is available to anyone receiving Social Security; its benefits for nursing home care are limited but its requirements are more stringent (thus some nursing homes will not accept Medicare patients).

What other insurance plans are accepted by the facility?

Is a charge made for doing personal laundry? May relatives handle this chore if they so choose?

What arrangements can be made for therapy? At what cost?

What limitations are there for personal items in the room—for example, a favorite chair, an extra chest of drawers, or a TV set? Can pictures be hung on the wall?

Are there restrictions on making or receiving telephone calls? Is a private telephone allowed?

Where is the resident's personal money kept? (Your parent needs some spending money for incidentals often available in the home and for offerings. Anna cannot handle cash, so we have a small discretionary "trust" fund set up for her with the bookkeeper; this pays for haircuts and other incidentals. Paul needs some cash in his wallet, but we never leave more than he or I could afford to lose.)

When was the facility last inspected by the appropriate city and state authorities?

Does the facility have a sprinkler system? How does the facility interpret "fire drill"? What special training is given to staff for such emergencies?

What are the regulations regarding smoking? Is it allowed in the dining room or in the residents' rooms? Are the staff allowed to smoke at desks or nursing stations? Or is smoking—for everyone—restricted to certain areas? Smoking regulations not only affect patients and visitors with respiratory ailments, but they affect fire safety as well.

Probe a bit about the work of the activities director. Ask to see a list of the preceding month's activities. Is there an active volunteer group or auxiliary?

Is there a resident chaplain, or a local pastor who regularly visits the facility? Is this permitted? What religious services or Bible classes are held or allowed?

Ask to see the menus for the past several days. Is a daily menu posted for residents to see? If you can, observe the serving of a noon meal—usually the biggest meal of the day. What provision is made for special diets or preferences (Paul dislikes pork, for example)? Is there ample variety of the primary food groups? Is the food prepared and served attractively?

Find Out Who's In Charge

Since the welfare of your loved one is involved, don't ever feel inhibited about asking questions. Carolyn and I have visited more than a dozen nursing homes, and it is our experience that the best ones will always welcome your questions, will give you all the time you want or need, will take you anywhere within the facility, and will not pressure you for an immediate decision. In fact, the better facilities welcome a return visit—with your parent if at all possible—so that other questions can be raised and answered before a final joint decision is made.

If anyone turns you off, if you are ever made to feel that you are intruding or meddling with your questions, then leave right away. Since you will likely be establishing a relationship of considerable duration, mutual trust and rapport must be established quickly if these are to flourish and continue.

By all means, try to see the administrator. He or she may not be able to give you all the time you need or want at that particular time (he may ask someone else to take you through the facility); however, you must make contact with the person in charge. You must see that his license and other qualifications are prominently displayed. You must have an opportunity to evaluate the style and character of the person who sets the tone for the entire facility. I mentioned earlier that I never met the administrator in Paul's first nursing home in Florida. Something is wrong with management if the chief administrator is always absent or seems reluctant to meet the public.

Experienced nursing home staff will tell you that adjustment to the nursing home environment usually takes three months. These are the crucial weeks during which you must have a good working relationship with the administrator, not merely with a subordinate. You will have new questions to ask about procedure. You may have complaints. It's better for staff morale and for your parent's well-being if you are able and free to go to the top to find answers and solutions.

Evaluate Nonprofit Facilities First

In your search for a nursing home, I suggest that you look first at church-related or other nonprofit facilities, if they exist in your area.

Nonprofit homes tend to have larger staffs and more extensive programs. Church-related facilities offer a dimension of "tender loving care" that commercial enterprises often don't.

Investigate Performance Expectations

Good nursing homes have high standards of performance and conduct for their staff. They provide training and orientation for newly employed staff. There will be evidence of some kind of continuing education for all staff.

One nursing home has the following paragraph in its statement of personnel policies and procedures.

The patient comes first. The patient is not an interruption of our work; he is the purpose of it. The patient is not someone with whom to argue or match wits. He is an important individual having feelings, emotions, prejudices, and wants. It is not only our job to care for his needs, but to contribute in every way to his comfort and happiness.

This same nursing home will fire employees for "soliciting or accepting tips" and for "physical or verbal abuse of patients." That kind of policy builds confidence.

Become Familiar With Residents' Rights

Nursing homes are required to provide new residents with a list of "patient's rights." Ask to see a copy. Here are a few examples of those rights.

● The patient is fully informed, by a physician, of his medical condition.

● He may participate in the planning of his medical treatment.

● The patient is transferred or discharged only for medical reasons.

● The patient is free from mental and physical abuse, and free from chemical and non-emergency physical restraints, except as authorized in writing by a physician for a specified and limited period of time, or when necessary to protect the patient from injury to himself or to others.

● He is treated with consideration, respect, and full recognition of his dignity and individuality, including privacy in treatment and in care for his personal needs.

● If married, the patient is assured privacy for visits by his or her spouse; if both are patients in the facility, they are permitted to share a room.

The Need to Monitor Nursing Home Care

Since policy is not always implemented, what can we do to insure continuing good care for our parents in nursing homes?

There is no substitute for personal observation and visits. Furthermore, I suggest that you observe the operation of the facility at different times of the day and week, with different staff on different shifts. Once you are recognized as the responsible person who is interested in your relative, it becomes easier to resolve problems.

You need to see your loved one at different times of day. If emotional or physical needs are not being met, this may cause your parent to become withdrawn or actively abusive.

Anna had difficulty with roommates during her first three months of nursing home residence. Her first companion emptied her dresser drawers as often as Anna did, and the inevitable mix-up of personal belongings brought them to literal blows. Her second roommate suffered from kleptomania. Anna's things kept disappearing—including her glasses and, once, even her false teeth. Nursing homes try to put compatible people together, but the process takes time. You and I need to be aware of what is really going on.

The quality of care and food needs to be monitored. There may be occasion to complain or to raise questions. However, your visits with administrative and supervisory staff ought not to be limited just to complaining. The more you visit the facility, the more you will wonder how the staff is able to cope as well as it does. A little affirmation and commendation goes a long way; there is precious little of it from patients, and not a great deal from patients' relatives.

Some of the better nursing home facilities plan for regular "family meetings," held at least quarterly, at which time senior staff, relatives, and patients (if they wish or can attend) meet together for sharing of news and concerns, for the raising of questions about procedures, or for suggestions for new programs or developments.

A few nursing homes have organized "resident councils" in which residents participate in some of the decision-making that affects their lives. There are physical limitations to such participation, but it is both good strategy and good management when such joint planning is allowed to happen.

Improving the Nursing Home "Community"

The nursing home environment can be improved; constructive suggestions can be made at family meetings or resident councils. Here are several ideas to ponder, whether you are choosing a home or trying to improve the one where your parent lives. Some ideas may only need *your* time and energy to implement.

1) *Pay the aides more money.* The people who do most of the work in nursing homes are the least educated, the least skilled, and the least paid. On-the-job training will help. However, standards won't be raised until wages rise. Higher pay scales might also help decrease the high turnover rate of nursing home employees.

2) *Provide patients with more sunshine and fresh air.* Safe patio areas can be added or incorporated with plans for new construction. Exits and entrances should be designed for ease of movement of handicapped persons; lighter-weight doors might be used. Aides or volunteers could assist residents with a bit of walking, or pushing a wheelchair outdoors, returning the patient indoors within a reasonable amount of time. On warmer days it would be a lot healthier for residents to sit in the sun than around a nurses' station.

I know of one nursing home that built a lovely fenced-in patio and equipped it with weatherproof furniture. But it is never used. The patio is accessible only through a gate outside the building; the architects forgot to include a doorway from inside the facility.

3) *Be creative with color.* Paint costs about the same, whether it's white or blue or orange or green. Many psychological studies, developed especially for industry, prove that certain colors are more restful than others. The drabness of nursing home facilities could be corrected with color. Varying the colors of rooms and corridors might help those patients who aren't color-blind find their hallway and their rooms more easily. Color-coding can also help.

4) *Provide nutritious snacks between meals.* Finger foods help digestion and might even reduce the need for daily laxatives. Carrot and celery sticks, slices of apple (with peelings removed for some), or other fruits and vegetables can help. More of these

fresh foods could be served with regular meals as well. It would take more time and perhaps more staff, but better health would result.

Usually raw vegetables and fresh fruit must be prepared so a patient can eat these and benefit from them; giving an apple or an orange to a patient who is partially paralyzed, who suffers from arthritis, or who wears loose dentures won't get this good food eaten.

5) *Add a bit of beauty.* Posters and reproductions of paintings dress up hallways and walls. They also provide "landmarks" as residents move through the facility. Large photomurals or scenic color panels printed as wallpaper can provide new "windows" in some of the larger rooms. Plants add lots of life and color.

Flower boxes on patios would brighten the area. Perhaps some of the residents could plant the seeds. It's exciting to watch things grow.

An aviary on a patio would require someone's special care and attention, but the color and sound of birds would brighten many lives. So would a small aquarium in the lobby or lounge of the nursing facility. Bird feeders and bird baths attract feathered friends, if someone keeps them filled with seed and water.

I often wish that pets were allowed in nursing homes, so patients could have something warm and cuddly to love. But at least we could arrange more pet shows. Children enjoy parading their pets, and residents enjoy a show-and-tell-and-touch time. Paul enjoys seeing Rascal, our German shepherd, whenever he visits us. And I've taken Rascal out to Paul's nursing home a few times—keeping her outdoors, of course. Rascal's cavorting has brought smiles to many faces.

Individual wall coverings could be placed behind or beside each bed to add beauty and individuality. It might be a simple framed picture, some needlepoint, or even something woven.

6) *Alter schedules to benefit the residents, not the staff.* Nursing homes operate much as hospitals do. Patients are awakened at 7:00 A.M. or even earlier. Often the staff begins serving the evening meal as early as 4:30 P.M., and patients are put to bed by 7:30 or 8:00. Why should it be so? There's lots of good television to be seen between 7:00 and 10:00 P.M.; such TV programs are important windows on the world for people who need all the

"reality orientation" they can get. It's denied them because of institutional dictum or tradition. Let people live while they live.

7) *Provide more living space.* Because construction costs are so high, space is costly. But only with adequate space can nursing homes truly be *homes.* Many smaller nursing homes being built today do not allow for enough public rooms. There isn't much opportunity for movement or group interaction when dining rooms double as activity rooms, and lobbies (often facing administrative offices) are the only lounges. It is the absence of adequate space, I believe, that accounts for much of the crowding of hallways and areas facing nurses' stations.

When building a new nursing home—or in modifying an older one—why not plan for *several* smaller rooms for activities? One could be used by ladies for sewing, another for crafts; disarray and even some messiness could be overlooked because these would be rooms for ongoing creative activity. Another room might be set aside for playing games. There might be *two* television viewing rooms in order to have at least two choices of channel at any given hour.

A larger multi-purpose room could be used for group exercises, programs, staff and resident council meetings, and resident talent shows. This larger room might also serve as the home's worship center. It should not be the dining room, where cooking odors permeate the air and kitchen staff are busy preparing food and setting tables.

I would also like to see architects pay more attention to the requirements of audio-visuals. They do this when designing schools and some churches. Films and filmstrips have proven their educational value; yet it is often impossible to darken the public rooms of nursing homes to show a movie or slides during daylight hours.

8) *Engineer better climate control.* Most of the newer facilities are air-conditioned. Some use individual heat-pump units similar to those found in motels. These can be regulated to suit individual preferences. However, handicapped or disoriented people either won't bother or they are unable to work the controls—or they will change them compulsively and erratically.

The slower metabolism of older people makes them much more susceptible to extreme changes of heat or cold without their showing the normal signs of sweating or shivering. And because they move about less, they often need a higher room temperature to survive. Hypothermia (dangerously low body temperature) is much more of a risk for persons past 65. Some constant temperature ought to be determined and maintained.

I'm also concerned that blankets be used at night. I see very few blankets around; most often a patient is covered only by a sheet or perhaps a bedspread. I suspect this is done because sheets and bedspreads are easier to launder than are blankets. Again, this procedure is based upon the convenience of the institution rather than upon the patient's needs. I've seen many nursing home residents, including Paul and Anna, huddled up because they are cold. Lightweight thermal blankets might be an economical and practical answer.

9) *Provide opportunities for learning.* Older people can and want to learn new things. Those who are more alert ought to have an opportunity to say what kind of curriculum they would like. Some may want to learn a new language or a new skill. Some may want to wrestle with the ideas of a new book. Others would enjoy serious Bible study. Authentic *classes* such as these could bring a new dimension of exciting growth to nursing home residents.

10) *Discover ways for residents to share with others.* The need to share is part of what keeps us human and caring.

Nursing home patients do not have much discretionary income; most of them are no longer able to contribute money to causes they would like to support or have supported in the past.

But there are other ways to share. They can serve as volunteers. They can sew or make simple toys for needy children at Christmastime. They can prepare mailings for the United Way or some other local charity. Rock-a-thons are organized to benefit the Heart Fund or other charities. Some residents adopt another more handicapped resident in the same home and find special ways to be helpful.

A nursing home in Minnesota operates a day-care center for children in its facilities. Many of the residents serve as honorary grandparents and are especially helpful with the very young. This interaction meets the needs of two generations.

11) *Incorporate more opportunities for spiritual involvement.* This

is especially important for secular commercial nursing homes to remember. Neighborhood churches can be enlisted to provide worship services. A retired pastor might serve as voluntary chaplain—with a regular visitation schedule and perhaps a weekly Bible class. Let music be part of the total environment. Church and school choirs might provide mini-concerts; children's choirs and handbell choirs would be well received. Hymn sings are popular.

Sacred music could be played over public address systems on Sunday mornings and perhaps, briefly, at bedtime. Classical or soothing popular music from the forties (which most residents would remember) could be played at other times. I wonder if some residents wouldn't try to sing more themselves if some older Mitch Miller "sing-along" records were played.

Opportunities for spiritual involvement could include many cultural programs. Local musicians could give concerts; one classical pianist received a federal arts grant to do just this in her city. High-school groups might present occasional one-act plays or puppet plays. Barbershop quartets would provide lots of fun and stir up happy memories.

12) *Consistently practice the principle of "team assessment."* This is an opportunity for all the staff—medical and social—to evaluate the progress and/or problems of individual patients. The activities director may have observed an attitude or a symptom the director of nursing needs to know about. The food services director (or a dining-room monitor) may have important impressions and information to share.

Here is where solutions to problems can be sought and tried out. Here is where serious commitment to rehabilitation can be demonstrated. Large nursing homes need the services of professional social workers to assist the institutional team, as well as to help patients and their families. Smaller nursing homes need social workers just as much, but might need to hire these on a part-time basis to begin with.

Many nursing homes already have incorporated several of these suggestions; in all these ways, nursing homes might provide more professional and more stimulating care.

Resources—Chapter 6

● Check the Address List at the end of this book for organizations concerned with administration of nursing homes and advocacy of residents' rights. Identify related or similar organizations in your own state.

● The *Consumer Survival Kit* is the publication of the television series aired on PBS. A current listing can be secured from the Maryland Center for Public Broadcasting, Owings Mills, MD 21117. One "kit" deals with nursing homes. Others highlight prescription and generic drugs, law, health insurance, and funeral planning.

Burger, Sarah Greene, and Martha D'Erasmo. *Living in a Nursing Home.* New York: Seabury Press, 1976.

Nursing Homes. Haldref Publications, 4000 Albemarle St. NW, Washington, D.C. 20016. This journal is edited for professionals in extended-care facilities and deals with governmental regulations, diet, architecture, rehabilitation, social services, and similar subjects.

7

Securing Professional Medical Care

The competent physician, before he attempts to give medicine to his patient, makes himself acquainted not only with the diseases which he wishes to cure, but also with the habits and constitution of the sick man.

—Cicero (106-43 B.C.)

A reliable and readily available family physician is an essential requirement, not only for you and your family but also for your parents and for those other older persons for whom you are responsible and concerned.

Since medical practices have changed radically over the past few years, securing appropriate and adequate medical help is a much greater problem than it once was. The medical clinic or complex has emerged. Specialization has increased. It has become difficult to know where and to whom to turn.

Questions to Ask

In our own search for medical care for Anna and Paul, I chose to ask these kinds of questions.

Would my present family physician accept an additional patient? Many physicians today are overloaded and are turning down new patients, so don't assume your doctor will be willing to care for your parent—ask.

Would my family physician accept an older patient? Does he or she have experience in geriatric medicine?

Lots of jokes are made about house calls, but find out if your physician still makes them. Emergencies do arise, and it isn't always possible to get a loved one to the doctor's office; besides, illnesses rarely jibe with established office hours. Find out whether your physician presently makes calls to nursing homes;

if not, would he do so? (Fortunately, our family doctor would accept new patients, did treat older people, did make calls to nursing homes, and would come to our home in an emergency.)

I would ask my doctor how he planned to monitor the quality of medical care of my parent in a nursing home. Professional staff within the nursing home must be consulted, of course, but a physician should not rely only on that one source of information.

When you do locate a physician for your parent, ask if he would prescribe generic brand drugs instead of the more expensive brand-name drugs, which are often produced by the same manufacturer.

Finding a Physician

If your present family physician can't or won't accept an additional patient, you will need to find someone who will. This person ought to be a general practitioner or someone active in "family practice" (a category you'll now find in the yellow pages under "physicians and surgeons"). The physician should have some experience in, or perhaps even specialize in, geriatric medicine.

How do you find your "leads"?

You can begin with the telephone directory, of course. However, I suggest you begin by asking some of your older retired friends whom they see about their medical problems. Doctors have reputations for empathy or for brusqueness, for caring or for cold professionalism. If possible, arrange for a personal interview. Although doctors may not like the idea, you are shopping for competence, compassion, and continuity. (In regard to this latter category, learn whether the doctor plans an early retirement. This might make a difference in your plans.)

Although a physician's professional ability and skill are not necessarily related to his or her faith, I appreciate a capable physician who is also a person of faith. Our family physician is a member of the church we attend. My urologist, who is also Paul's, was willing to pray before he operated on me for kidney stones; I like that. My dermatologist, who is also Paul's, is a devout Jew, and the rapport that grows out of mutual respect and understanding for God's power goes beyond any immediate medical problem.

Special Medical People

You will need specialists for special needs. Your regular family doctor will make recommendations as needed, but let me cite some of the specialists we have had to consult.

I had never heard of a physiatrist until Paul had his stroke, or CVA (cerebrovascular accident). A physiatrist specializes in physical medicine and rehabilitation, including muscular treatment. This science grew out of recent wars, when severely wounded and disabled veterans required special care and rehabilitation. While it is still a developing science, its lessons and procedures are helping countless accident (including burn) victims of all ages.

Physiatrists prescribe the type, kind, and length of various therapies that are then carried out by physical, occupational, and speech therapists. Older persons with stroke or heart problems, or those with muscular or arthritic difficulties, may benefit from such specialized help.

We needed a urologist for Paul. Many older males develop prostate problems—my father died of prostate cancer. Blockages and strictures may require dilation. It used to be said that pneumonia was the ultimate killer, but antibiotics have changed that. Urinary-tract or kidney infections have now replaced pulmonary infections as a leading cause of death among the elderly, both male and female.

We also needed to find a dermatologist (a skin specialist) for Paul. Our family physician was suspicious of a discoloration on Paul's scalp; it turned out to be malignant. A dermatologist successfully treated Paul's condition; in fact, the "operation" was performed in his office. Dermatologists also help in treating fungus, dry skin conditions (especially bothersome to older people during colder months), and athlete's foot. They remove warts and other surface growths.

Anna required a neurologist to diagnose the status of her brain and nervous system. Later, she needed an orthopedic surgeon to repair her broken hip.

Hearing may have to be checked and impacted wax removed. Otologists are ear specialists. Some doctors still specialize in ear, nose, and throat disorders.

Eyes deteriorate with age and should be tested regularly. Glaucoma is a special risk for the elderly. An *optometrist* examines eyes for vision and prescribes glasses. An *ophthalmologist* also examines eyes and prescribes glasses, but he is a medical doctor who can diagnose and treat diseases of the eye and perform surgery. An *optician* fills prescriptions and grinds lenses for glasses.

Anna now has serious problems with her toenails, and I hear this is a problem for many older people. Nursing home staff are reluctant to cut toenails because so many older people are diabetic or borderline diabetic, and the risk of cutting into a toe is grave. Thus, you may be asked to secure a specialist—a podiatrist (they used to be called chiropodists)—to do this chore.

Dental Needs

You'll need to find a dentist. Older people's teeth should be checked, cleaned, and maintained as regularly as ours should. If older persons wear dentures, these also should be checked from time to time. If they slip, they can be tightened. Periodically, dentures need a thorough cleaning with the kind of equipment available in a dental office. Dentures may require repair—and repair is often possible.

Sometimes an older person's gums recede to the point that dentures cannot be kept in place. This has happened to Anna's lower gum, so she uses only an upper denture, mostly for aesthetic reasons, and that with increasing rarity.

Dentists may make visits to nursing homes, bringing portable equipment for routine maintenance of teeth and dentures or for making molds for new dentures.

I'll be explaining the differences between Medicare and Medicaid in a later chapter. However, if your parent is eligible for Medicaid assistance (which includes dental care, unlike Medicare), be sure your dentist will accept Medicaid payments; many will not. (Some doctors and hospitals won't either, so they should be asked, too.)

Securing Professional Medical Care

Medical Transportation

It may not be necessary for your parent who lives in a nursing home to leave the facility for medical treatment. Physicians are expected to visit nursing home patients. In fact, Medicaid patients are to be visited *monthly.* Although nursing homes do not have X-ray equipment, portable mobile X-ray units can be summoned as needed. At a physician's request, laboratories will also send technicians to the nursing home (or to your home) for blood and specimen tests.

Ambulances cost forty dollars or more per trip within city limits. If your doctor believes an emergency requires an ambulance, by all means call an ambulance service if your parent is at home, or agree to this quickly when the nursing home calls you. However, for routine visits to doctors or dentists—and sometimes to emergency rooms in hospitals—drive your parent yourself. It's probably more reassuring, and it is obviously more economical.

If available in your area, a "medicab" or a minibus provided for handicapped people by your local bus service could also be called.

Paul's nurse's aide, Juanita, called us one day in great agitation. Paul was suffering chest pains, and she felt he was having a heart attack. Our doctor was on vacation, but his associate said to bring Paul to the emergency room of a local hospital, where he would meet us. As things turned out, Paul merely had a bad case of indigestion. Of course, no one wants to take chances where chest pains are concerned. But in this case I'm glad we didn't call for an ambulance.

Other Forms of Medical Care

There may be times when you'll need a Registered Nurse (R.N.) or a Licensed Practical Nurse (L.P.N.). Often an experienced paramedic or nurse's aide can provide the special health care required. Consult your public health agency or a professional referral service. The next chapter offers suggestions about hiring such help.

However, medical care as such may not always be needed.

Handicapped people aren't sick—they're handicapped. Disoriented people aren't ill—they're merely confused. Perhaps only a companion or a "sitter" is required.

Whatever the physical state of your parent, you'll probably feel more secure and competent about home health care if you take the time to learn some of the basics. Books and guides may be purchased at your bookstore or borrowed from your public library. The Red Cross periodically offers courses in first aid and in home health care; you will find these invaluable.

The techniques of turning and bathing patients in bed, and changing bed linens with a patient in the bed are skills that can be learned and used in many different kinds of situations.

And when medical help is needed, it's available in quantity and quality. We are blessed.

8

###

Hints on Hiring
for Home Health Care

In order that people may be happy in their work,
these three things are needed:
They must be fit for it;
They must not do too much of it;
And they must have a sense of success in it.
—John Ruskin (1819-1900)

Carolyn and I soon came to the realization that we (and others of our family who lived in Austin) could not care for Anna (and later, for Paul) all by ourselves.

We had to find help.

When you arrive at that point, remember that there are many different ways of caring for invalid or handicapped parents at home. They are costly, but one has to compare these costs with those of nursing homes.

When husband and wife both work outside the home, someone needs to be at home to be the *caretaker* and *caregiver.* Even when only one spouse leaves home to work, the other needs time off from health care for home care. And both spouses need time off for themselves. They must recognize that the decision to provide home care for a parent literally means providing twenty-four-hour-a-day care. I'll return to this point later.

Levels of Care

Except in severe illnesses, a full-time registered nurse will not be required. In such cases, a hospital or a skilled nursing facility ought to be considered. For occasional medical needs, such as giving injections or other medication, special arrangements can be made with a private R.N., a nursing service agency, or the public health program in your area.

Frequently, an L.P.N. (Licensed Practical Nurse) or L.V.N.

(Licensed Vocational Nurse) can perform many of the same medical services at a lower hourly rate. Another less expensive alternative, when patients do not require frequent medical attention, is to hire a *nurse's aide*—a paramedical person trained in providing more limited care for handicapped and bedridden persons. Aides can cope with the special requirements of patient hygiene. They can check blood pressure and give enemas. They can exercise muscles and assist a handicapped person in walking. Aides do not give injections, but they are permitted to administer other medication on schedule.

If no serious medical problems exist but your parent is basically disoriented and confused, you might hire an *adult sitter* or companion.

These four types of persons can be hired through professional medical employment agencies or pools. Look for these under the "nurses' registries" category in your telephone book. Hiring a person through an agency will cost more per hour, but eliminates the need for handling the detailed paperwork of withholding taxes and Social Security.

For those with limited financial resources, reimbursement for some of these services—including homemaker or "chore care" services—may be available through your welfare agency.

Therapists

Physical, occupational, and speech therapists may be hired on a per-visit basis in your home—or you can arrange to transport your parent to clinics established for this purpose. Mental health centers sometimes provide therapists through outreach programs.

Your Accountability to the Federal Government

If you decide not to hire someone through an agency, you must prepare yourself for some bookkeeping tasks. First you need to apply to the Internal Revenue Service for an "employer identification number." This can be in your name or in your parent's name; I chose to apply in Paul's name.

Your employee must fill out a W-4 form upon being hired, indicating Social Security number and the number of exemptions claimed. You will file these forms; they authorize you to make deductions for withholding taxes and Social Security taxes. As an employer, you share in Social Security payments; obtain current schedules from the IRS or your local Social Security office.

You must file quarterly statements with the IRS, remitting the tax money you have withheld. Your remittance to the IRS includes both withholding taxes and Social Security (your employee's and your portion). You will make an annual report to the Social Security Administration on the total amount you sent during the year through the IRS. If you receive additional forms from the IRS during the year, check to see if you must complete these. Employers of household help are not expected to file the extensive reports required of others, but once you have an employer's identification number and are on the computer, you may receive more forms than you need to fill out.

Prior to January 31 of each year, you must provide W-2 report forms to each person you employed during the previous year.

I used bookkeeping pads for my records. Twelve columns per page worked best for me, but you will develop your own system and work with your own tools. Once I got organized, I found that it took me fifteen to twenty minutes a week to enter the data and make out the checks. It probably took me longer because our aide did not work a standard forty-hour week; each week was different, mostly because my own schedule so often involved travel away from home. Also, with each change in the tax law or Social Security (FICA), new withholding schedules were issued and everything had to be refigured.

I must add, however, that my very simple accounting procedures worked adequately for me. My records allowed me to make out quarterly reports and annual statements quickly and easily.

Practical Considerations: Pay and Expectations

You'll probably want to pay at least the minimum hourly wage. You may have to match what the employee would receive through a nursing pool or agency (not what you pay the agency, which then makes its own deductions). You'll need to agree on payments for overtime or holidays, if you expect this from your employee. You'll need to agree on sick leave and vacation time. You'll need to determine how often you will consider periodic pay increases.

In our case, we paid an hourly rate slightly above the minimum wage and decided that because of inflation we would raise that rate after six months, probably increasing the rate annually thereafter. We allowed paid sick leave to accrue at the rate of one day for each month worked, and promised a vacation of two weeks with pay, beginning after one year of employment.

In evaluating a potential employee, you'll want to determine your own criteria. In our situation we considered such things as experience, compatibility (both with Paul and with us), empathy with older people, personal habits and appearance, ability to drive, willingness to cook occasionally, ability to read out loud with enjoyment, and some interest in crafts.

An Example: Juanita

Juanita Sanders came as an answer to our prayers. She enjoyed older people. She and Paul hit it off immediately; it helped that both spoke Spanish as well as English. Juanita was a careful driver; she took Paul in his old Dodge to the rehabilitation clinic for therapy. Later, when therapy ended, she drove him to a day activities center two or three times a week.

Juanita was interested in what the various therapists were doing; she wanted to improve her own skills for future cases, so what she observed she practiced at home with Paul. She was excited about the kinds of exercises demonstrated at the activities center—and again, she followed through with these at home, as well as walking daily with Paul.

She took pride in his appearance. His daily shave and shower became a ritual. She sensed that he liked to wear a tie with his shirt. She recognized his need for personal dignity, perhaps as a respected *patrón*.

She practiced what she heard and saw of speech therapy. We chuckled at some of her pronunciations, but she meant well and she loved to read to Paul. She read the Bible in English and Spanish; Paul would usually point to the passage he wanted read.

They also read books. Juanita became a fan of Corrie ten Boom; she read more of Corrie's writings on her own time, and made it a point to see the film *The Hiding Place* when it came to Austin. In time, she made her own public profession of faith, largely due to the things she had read to Paul.

Juanita was not only a good nurse's aide; she was also a responsible companion. When it seemed possible and feasible for Paul to travel to Florida for a one-month Christmastime reunion with his two brothers and a sister, we had no qualms about Juanita accompanying him on the plane and continuing her care of him in Florida.

Juanita is approaching her own time of retirement. She has been ill twice. The first time, she had trouble with her knee and was suffering from exhaustion. We insisted that she add vacation time to her sick leave. Because of the commitments Carolyn and I both had at that time, we placed Paul in a nursing home for one month. Paul understood that it was a short-term arrangement and a respite both for Juanita and for us, and he cooperated fully.

Juanita's second illness was more serious. After her return from Florida, she developed a new problem with her knee. For a time, it seemed she would need surgery. Because Juanita is a diabetic, her doctor wanted to avoid an operation. Finally he insisted she find a "lighter" case. Reluctantly, we all agreed this was essential.

During the next twelve weeks we had three substitutes. Carolyn and I alternated working full-time at home, exhausting our own sick leave. We could not find a suitable new aide and companion, and we had become exhausted. The time had come to find an alternative. Paul shared in the decision to find a good nursing home.

It's Your Time and Your Home

Home care is a glorious proposition, but it is costly—in dollars and cents and in energy and life-style.

When you add up everything you pay for a visiting R.N. or L.P.N., plus wages for a nurse's aide or companion, your monthly total will probably equal or surpass what nursing home care would cost. Saving money, of course, isn't the reason you may opt for home care.

Remember, also, that there are 168 hours in a week. At most, you will hire someone during the daytime hours—perhaps for 45 hours a week. That leaves 123 hours per week for which *you* are responsible, in addition to your own regular work at home or away from home.

Many of those 123 hours will be nighttime hours, usually occupied with sleep. But Carolyn and I, who chose home care for more than two years, can testify that very few nights are filled with total, peaceful slumber—much like the nights when Paul and Anna cared for *us* as newborns. Only now, you are conscious of moans and groans instead of childish wails. You get up at least once to check on whether your parent is covered, whether a catheter is still attached, or whether your parent is still breathing.

Paul shared breakfast with us, which meant that we wakened him and got him up. Juanita arrived during breakfast. Usually, all of us were back home in time to share supper together. Our weekends were given over entirely to Paul's care, as we did all the things Juanita normally did Monday through Friday.

And of course, Carolyn or I put Paul to bed every night, except for those weekends when we slipped away. We learned we had to take mini-breaks once every six or seven weeks.

Perhaps this sounds like martyrdom. It wasn't. We consciously chose to do what we did. We were glad we were able to involve ourselves and our lives with Paul in this way. We were often tired and frustrated, but I think we sensed more of the sweet than we did of the bitter.

What I must emphasize, however, is that the decision to provide home care must be a careful and conscious decision to commit yourself, your mate, and any children still living at home to caring for your parent. The involvement will be total and comprehensive.

Unless you are able to afford around-the-clock help, you will be responsible for at least two-thirds of every week. This will affect all your relationships, inside and outside the home. It will affect activities, hobbies, and leisure time. It will affect other members of the family. It will affect your marriage.

Dr. Rita Rogers described some of this at the 1980 meeting of the American Psychiatric Association. She said that it takes a mature partner in a healthy marriage to accept the situation and provide the necessary support and comfort. Old rivalries among children are often revived when it's time to care for an elderly parent. The question of which child the parent liked best may resurface.

Spanning these tensions is the impact of time and the physical presence of another adult.

You will have to decide whether home care is the best way for you to go.

We believed it was the preferred alternative for us. It was best for Anna as long as she was able to cope with semi-independent living. It was excellent for Paul, because only in this way was he able to benefit from the three kinds of therapy that have equipped him for his new limited independence in a fine nursing home.

Home care takes its toll of energy. It can reward you, however, with renewed relationships with loved ones and with the discovery of the true nature of compassion. You may not always be ecstatic nor enthusiastic about this new relationship, but there are many times when you will be enormously satisfied.

Resources—Chapter 8

● Check durable medical supply houses and the Sears catalog for items that will make home care more professional and easy.

● Urinals (for male and female use), bedpans, elevating tables for use at bedside, sturdy trapezes to help a patient lift himself, and similar items are readily available. So are a variety of blood-pressure instruments and pulse-rate monitors. Some of these are the electronic digital type, which anyone can learn to use.

● Hospital supply houses will sell to private individuals catheters, drainage bags, pads, and rubber sheeting for beds.

9

*Transporting Your
Handicapped Parent*

> *I wandered today to the hill, Maggie,*
> *To watch the scene below,*
> *The creek and the old rusty mill, Maggie,*
> *As we used to, long ago.*
> —George Washington Johnson (1858-1917)

Whether your handicapped parent lives with you or in a nursing home facility, there will be many times when you will want to go out for a drive. Often there is a need to visit a doctor or dentist, and transportation becomes a necessity. At other times, the trip is merely for a change of scene and pace, for shopping, for a meal out, or for some special celebration or excursion.

Transporting a handicapped parent isn't difficult, but it is different from anything you may have experienced previously. You need to be aware of these differences, plan ahead, and overcome your understandable hesitancy and fear. Soon you will realize that in this area, too, "practice makes perfect," or at least it will make things more comfortable for both you and your parent.

I still shudder at the memory of our first excursion with Paul, when he was living in the nursing home in Florida. Carolyn and I decided to drive him to a nature walk we had heard about. We thought he'd enjoy seeing and hearing the birds, as well as again observing some typical tropical vegetation. It was my first experience in helping an invalid from a wheelchair into a car seat, and I hoped Paul wouldn't notice how nervous I was. When we arrived at our destination, I saw six steps and no ramps—and I had never negotiated a wheelchair over steps. It was a bumpy ride for Paul, but Carolyn was there to help, and the three of us learned from the experience.

Moving From Wheelchair to Car

Let's look first at the maneuver of *transfer*. The technique is useful and necessary not only for transferring a person from wheelchair to car seat, but also from wheelchair to bed or wheelchair to dining room chair, and vice versa.

The nature of the disability determines how the maneuver is carried out. Your parent may be frail or stiff-jointed from arthritis or the aftermath of an operation. Since her hip fracture, Anna is in this condition. A *paraplegic* is paralyzed from the waist down, but usually has developed strong arm muscles. A *quadriplegic* is paralyzed from the neck down and cannot use any limbs. A *hemiplegic* is paralyzed on one side of the body and cannot use the leg and arm on that side (Paul is a hemiplegic.)

If your parent still walks, even minimally, and is able to stand, both of you can more easily effect the maneuver. Provide some support, perhaps an arm under the shoulder, to assist your parent to sit comfortably. You will likely need to help place his or her legs inside the car.

A hemiplegic requires a bit more support and help. Once the person is standing and holding onto the roof of the car or the car door, move the wheelchair away so you can stand beside him. Provide underarm support and also hold onto his waist, gripping the belt or side. Help the person to turn or pivot and assist him with seating; then help him to pivot again so he faces forward. Lift his legs during this maneuver. Exiting is the reverse of this procedure.

A paraplegic soon learns to accomplish this maneuver on his own. You've doubtless seen many such disabled persons driving specially equipped cars. They remove one of the side arms of the wheelchair and put those strong arm muscles to use, grabbing the steering wheel or seat belt to pull or slide themselves onto the seat. I've often been amazed to see a paraplegic go on to fold his wheelchair, lift it, and place it inside the car.

A quadriplegic is usually transported by van while still seated in a wheelchair. Otherwise, a person with this kind of disability has to be lifted up and onto another seat or bed. A strong person can do it by placing an arm under the knees and another under the shoulders, but this maneuver is more easily performed by two people. A plastic board is sometimes used to aid the sliding maneuver from wheelchair to car seat.

These various transfer maneuvers are illustrated and described in pamphlets available through your local Heart Association office.

Don't be afraid to begin to learn how to best handle another human body. Not everyone is fragile, and you and your parent will learn as you practice the procedure. Your objective is comfort within the bounds of safety—your parent's and your own.

You'll learn where it's best for you to stand, how to brace yourself, how much support to give your loved one, where exactly to place the wheelchair for entry or exit, when to raise the footrests of the wheelchair, and so on.

If your parent is disoriented as well as disabled, you will have to repeat the instructions or the steps of what you are doing. Gently give instructions about when to stand, where to grab, when to pivot, and when to sit.

When making transfers in the home—from wheelchair to a chair, for example—choose a sturdy chair with arms, if possible. If you transfer a person to a straight-backed chair without arms, it's helpful to have a sturdy table or a walker close by for additional support.

It's also a good idea to check that the wheels of the wheelchair are locked, especially during transfer maneuvers. And always use the car seat belt for your parent as well as for yourself.

Maneuvering and Hauling the Wheelchair

It will often be necessary for you to push the wheelchair. Stairs and curbs are difficult to negotiate, as are some doors—particularly into rest rooms. You'll soon learn (often by making mistakes) what works best for you.

When I approach a curb from the street, I push down on the arms of the wheelchair to lift up the front wheels; once those front wheels are on the curb (and sidewalk), I lift up and push. When returning to street level, I walk backwards, with my feet on the street and the wheelchair on the sidewalk. I push down on the wheelchair arm, pulling the patient with me and rolling the wheelchair down the curb on the big wheels. Once we're at street level, I gently lower the front of the wheelchair. There's a balance or pivot point in maneuvering a wheelchair that makes movement more easy, once you discover the knack.

Everyone pushes up inclines. Some folks prefer to walk backwards down an incline, bracing themselves against the weight of the wheelchair and patient.

Never attempt to go through a revolving door or walk on an escalator with a wheelchair. Find a convenient side door. Multistory buildings all have readily accessible elevators. You may have to hunt for an elevator in a shopping mall, but there is one somewhere.

Usually you will transport the wheelchair with you. If you do this often, you'll appreciate a lighter-weight unit that allows armrests and footrests to be removed or folded. In a four-door sedan, you may prefer to place the folded wheelchair upright on the floor in front of the back seat. Most often, it will be more practical to place the wheelchair in the trunk—but this requires lifting. Be sure your trunk lid closes easily once the wheelchair is inside.

A wheelchair carrier has been designed that looks something like a bicycle carrier and attaches to the rear bumper of the car. This particular carrier (brand name: *Tilt n Tote*) tilts to the ground. You merely roll the folded wheelchair into place and raise and lock the carrier. It costs about $250. Bike carriers can be adapted for transporting wheelchairs, and they cost much less; in fact, some manufacturers make a special unit for wheelchairs. Of course, you will still have to lift the wheelchair when using a bicycle carrier, but you might find this easier than the constant lifting in and out of automobile trunks. Keep in mind that transporting a wheelchair outside the car will subject it to weather and possible theft.

You'll save energy and some hassle if you telephone ahead to see if the doctor's or dentist's office already has a wheelchair you could borrow upon your arrival. A few department stores and shopping malls now offer this public service as well. I wish more churches did.

A Car or a Van?

What kind of vehicle is best for transporting handicapped persons?

Just about any car except the smallest compacts will do. I was pleasantly surprised to discover that my mid-sized Mercury Zephyr has more leg and head room than Paul's old gas-guzzling Dodge Polara. You do need to be sure you're buying enough leg room and a large enough trunk (or storage area, in a station wagon) for a wheelchair.

Some families invest in a van. Although such vehicles sit higher off the ground than regular automobiles, middle seats can be removed and the wider doors may allow direct transporting of a patient without transferring from a wheelchair, if some sort of ramp is used. A sturdy ramp could be made from half-inch or thicker *exterior*-grade plywood, and it would help to attach some kind of hook device on the end of the ramp that will meet the van floor. Check with truck body supply houses for such hardware. Also check the height of side van doors carefully before you make a purchase; you want to be sure there is enough head room for the patient during transfer.

Hydraulic lifts raise the patient and wheelchair from ground level to van floor level without the use of a ramp. You can secure information about such devices from taxi and bus companies that use them, or from state rehabilitation or welfare offices who serve the disabled. A category to check in your yellow pages might be "handicapped—mobile aids." Hydraulic and all-electric lifts are priced between two and three thousand dollars. A folding aluminum ramp that fits into the side stairwell of a van will cost around eight hundred dollars installed.

Some provision must be made in vans for securing the wheelchair firmly to the floor during transporting. Taxis or buses that transport wheelchair patients commercially install a sturdy safety-lock device that is bolted to the floor and secures the wheelchair with a heavy pin. Inspect these devices yourself. An extra seat belt should be installed, or an accessory seat belt designed for use with wheelchairs could be purchased.

Some recreational vehicles may adapt themselves to the transportation of handicapped persons. However, most RV doors are narrow. Strategically placed grab bars would help, as would some sort of removable ramp; walking an incline would likely be easier than stepping up or down.

Transporting Your Handicapped Parent

Public Transportation

Many metropolitan bus systems offer special transportation to handicapped persons, as do some taxi companies. The vehicles are specially adapted vans or minibuses, with raised roofs and hydraulic or electric lifts. Wheelchairs are firmly locked to the vehicle floor. Taxi fares may have a surcharge. City bus fares will also be higher because the service provided is door-to-door, but charges will be lower than taxi fares. Hours of service may be limited. Investigate the services that might be available in your area. If not available, this might be a service idea to promote.

The Need for a Change of Scene

Anna seems reluctant now to leave the nursing home; perhaps she senses a kind of security there that she doesn't wish disturbed. However, I was able to entice her to go for drives three times last year. I picked warm, sunny days or days of special significance. One such day was Mother's Day, and it made me feel especially good to be able to do something different and special with her on this particular day.

Once we just drove around town, looking at houses and trees and clouds. Another time we drove fifteen miles out of town to one of Austin's lovely lakes. It was a beautiful drive, but it was too lengthy for Anna. She became increasingly nervous and, I thought, even frightened. A third time, we drove to a nearby shopping center that has a year-round ice-skating rink. Anna enjoyed watching the youngsters learn to skate.

Paul, on the other hand, is delighted to travel whenever we have the time or the inclination. We take him to church every two or three weeks. We go to cafeterias to enjoy a greater selection of food than he normally has. We've made several all-day excursions. Once we drove thirty miles to Bastrop State Park, which is famous for its "Lost Pines" forest. We've been to Aquarena Springs in San Marcos, also some thirty miles away, where Paul was able to take the glass-bottom boat trip. We drove to the LBJ Ranch and National Park and toured the ranch in National Park Service buses; that was seventy miles away. We've made several trips to San Antonio (eighty miles away) to see the zoo,

97

Institute of Texan Cultures, and San Antonio's Old Town *mercado,* or market. These excursions were especially good fun because they often included a picnic and other family members.

Now that Carolyn and I have graduated from our tent-type camping to our first travel trailer (a thirteen-footer!), we're looking forward to experimenting with some one-day excursions with Paul. We think that being able to have a meal on site, having a place to stretch out for a nap, and having a portable toilet close by may make such excursions more pleasant.

Our longest trip with Paul by auto was to the Dallas-Fort Worth airport, some 200 miles away. We had arranged for Paul and Juanita to travel to Orlando to spend the month of December with a brother and sister who lived there. Another brother would be coming down from Pittsburgh, so there was a real family reunion and many opportunities to meet with old friends who lived in Florida or who were visiting there during the winter. Paul's doctor said he could make the trip, and Juanita went along to help. Boarding the plane in Dallas-Fort Worth seemed best because there was a direct flight from there to Orlando. We met the flight there upon their return.

Air Travel

Airlines are cooperative and helpful with handicapped passengers. Usually they require that someone travel with the disabled person. They will allow for early boarding at the gate (as well as debarkation) with the airline's wheelchair, providing you ask for this service in advance. They will check your wheelchair and walker as regular baggage. One is not required to go first class to receive these services.

Always Plan Ahead

Any trip—short or long—requires advance planning.

For example, barrier-free easy access and availability of adequate rest room facilities for handicapped persons are essential criteria for us. We have a listing of eating places in Austin that provide barrier-free access, but we often telephone ahead to ask specific questions about ramps, rest room facilities, and special parking arrangements.

There is a church we now visit only rarely, even though it is Paul's denomination. Its only access is through an entrance that has three steps. The steps are high and shallow, so the only way to enter is for two people actually to lift Paul in his wheelchair up the stairs and into the foyer. New pews were recently installed, and in order to accommodate more people the aisles were narrowed. A wheelchair can no longer be maneuvered around corners and pews, which means Paul must leave his wheelchair in the foyer and walk, with walker, to the nearest accessible seat. Rest rooms in this church are in the basement, which is reached from the sanctuary only by walking down a *circular* stairway.

One cafeteria we no longer patronize has delicious food, but it is impossible to get into the men's room with a wheelchair. One door opens into a narrow corridor, where the entrances to the men's and women's rest rooms are located. Entering this second door from the narrow passageway with a wheelchair is almost impossible. The rest room itself contains no grab bars for the handicapped.

On the other hand, it is a joy to take Paul to the new Special Events Center at the University of Texas. Specially designed areas are reserved for the handicapped. There is plenty of room for wheelchairs, and folding chairs are brought in for attendants. The sight line is superb. The center has plenty of ramps, elevators, and barrier-free rest rooms.

Incidentally, we've discovered that all of the newer rest stops on interstate highways are also barrier-free.

I may seem to be obsessed with bathrooms, but the availability of appropriate rest rooms, no matter how far you travel, is of great importance and must be part of your planning. I even keep a plastic urinal in the trunk for emergencies that do occur.

Savor the Moments

Enjoy the adventure of traveling with your handicapped parent. The opportunities for exciting change—for both of you—are many. The trips don't have to be long. With experience and planning, your effort will go a long way to add some spice and adventure to all of your lives.

10

❖

Comfort Care: Personal Hygiene and Grooming

Darling, I am growing old,
Silver threads among the gold
Shine upon my brow today;
Life is fading fast away.
—E. E. Rexford (1848-1916)

Older people may sometimes give the impression that they no longer care about personal appearance. For a few, this is likely due to carelessness or listlessness. For many, however, I think it may be failing eyesight or a physical handicap that restricts one's personal grooming.

Cleanliness is important, both for the patient's health and for the comfort of others. Odors are caused by being bedridden, by loss of bladder and bowel control, and perhaps by a faster rate of dying cells as well as a metabolic change. The only solution is frequent bathing and frequent change of clothes and bed linens.

Bathing and Showering

Nursing home staff do try to change soiled clothing and bed linen with some regularity. Most nursing homes have a requirement that staff sponge-bathe patients whenever soiling occurs. However, Paul and Anna are showered only twice a week, and their hair isn't always shampooed with each shower.

Nursing homes have bathtubs, often with sophisticated whirlpool attachments for massage and therapy. However, these are used only when ordered or prescribed by the attending physician.

Home care provides an opportunity for more frequent attention to personal hygiene. We encouraged a daily shower when Anna lived with us; after she moved into the retirement residence facility, we tried to include a weekly bath when she visited us. Paul also received a daily shower when he lived in our home. Because of his paralysis and weight, we were unable to provide him with the enjoyment of a soaking bath.

Hydraulic swivel bath chairs lower a patient into a bathtub, as low as two inches from the bottom. Shower chairs of several types are available through durable medical goods stores. Some of the massage-type shower heads—preferably the kind with extension hoses—would add variety and perhaps relaxation to the shower.

I have often wished for the European-type of bidet, both for home care and in nursing homes. Substituting a hand-held shower head for your regular one helps in showering a person who is handicapped and is seated in the bathtub (on one of the special stools available for this purpose). Installing an extra-long length of shower hose to reach the commode would serve the purpose of a bidet.

Living With Incontinence

Accept the fact that accidents will happen. One dictionary defines *incontinence* as "inability of the body to control the evacuative functions." It isn't planned, it isn't deliberate, and it's never a reason for scolding.

Since incontinence is a major cause of bad odor, do what you can to help a patient with this problem. We provided a portable commode at bedside. We encourage use of the bathroom before leaving home (or nursing home) for a visit to church, doctor, or restaurant. We tried to minimize nighttime accidents. This is more easily accomplished with male patients, since their catheters are used externally. Talk with your doctor about catheter needs for male and female patients.

Protect furniture and beds with pads, change clothing, sponge bathe, and use lots of powder and deodorant. It isn't easy for children to care for their parents in this very private and personal way, but it is a necessity with no other alternative. It can become a loving service if you handle this unavoidable aspect of living tactfully, patiently, and professionally.

Provide your parent with an adequate supply of underwear. You might want to consider using protective liners and pads, if incontinence is constant. Pads may be purchased least expensively in boxes of two hundred or three hundred, depending upon size, through hospital equipment and supply houses.

Skin and Nail Care

While this is not particularly a matter of personal hygiene, we've found that a few drops of bath or baby oil on a damp washcloth, rubbed onto the back, arms, and calves helps the patient feel more comfortable during colder months and combats psoriasis.

Give special attention to hands and nails. Carolyn and I try always to carry a pre-moistened towelette and nail clippers with file whenever we visit Anna or Paul. Both often require special hand and nail care. Since Anna now eats mostly with her fingers, clean hands are a matter of health.

Attention to Hair

Don't overlook hair care. Hair should be shampooed with each shower. Oils build up on the scalp, and the scalp needs to be kept clean.

Hair care also includes consideration of the appropriate coiffure.

Anna had beautiful long hair that she sometimes braided, but more often wore in a bun. As her disorientation increased, she would constantly rearrange her hair. It became a frenetic activity—removing and losing hairpins, tying the long hair into knots, and never really combing or brushing it. It was sad to see her try to braid her once-beautiful hair; she had forgotten how to do it.

Carolyn and I decided that cutting her hair would probably be best for her. One of the nursing home aides first suggested it. Anna had never visited a beautician in her life, but this was another of those "parenting decisions" we had to make. We didn't think she would be sufficiently patient or quiet to go through the process of getting a permanent, so we chose a short bob and arranged to have her hair cut every six or eight weeks. Now her hair is too short to knot, and it is easy to comb. For women less disoriented than my mother, a regular visit to the beauty shop could become a highlight of the week or month. Most nursing homes set aside a room that doubles as both beauty and barber shop, with licensed people providing services once or twice a week. Costs are much lower than in commercial shops.

I cut Paul's hair. We bought a barbering outfit when my sons were little boys, and I cut their hair until they were in their early teens and began to complain. The older barbering outfit seems to work well enough, and Paul doesn't have too much hair left anyway. There is a barber shop in Paul's nursing home, but he refuses to use it. Whatever his reason, I take this as a small vote of confidence.

Oral Hygiene

If possible, let your parent continue the oral aspect of personal hygiene by brushing teeth or soaking dentures.

If your parent isn't able to manage this task, you or the nursing staff will have to see that it's done. Dentures should be soaked each night in some kind of cleaning agent. They should be brushed with a stronger denture cleaner periodically. Mechanical denture cleaners are also available for home use. If your parent has natural teeth, assist in brushing them. He or she also might want to use some kind of mouthwash.

If your parent lives in a nursing home, you will need to provide toothpaste, denture powder or cleaning tablets, mouthwash, a denture container, powder, bath oil, shaving cream and lotion, and some sort of razor. (An electric razor is preferable.)

Label items with your parent's name. Use a waterproof marker for powder, scratch or etch name or initials onto an electric razor, or write the name on masking tape and affix it to items.

Clothes Do Help Morale

You'll need to provide a sufficient change of clothing for your parent, probably more than was used in "normal" times. The clothing should be attractive and appropriate. Buy colors your parent enjoys; there's no need to be drab or dull. Appropriateness refers to the weather or climate control of the nursing home as well as to your parent's modesty needs.

Laundry can be done at the nursing home; sometimes it's

included in the overall fee, or there may be an extra charge. If you choose to launder your parent's clothing yourself, plan to do this at least twice a week, as clothing must be changed often. Whether laundry is done at the nursing home or in your home, clothes will wear out faster than usual. High-strength industrial detergents are used in institutional laundries, and clothing is soiled and washed more often.

You'll probably want to choose more *washable* clothing. Retain one or two more formal outfits for special occasions, but remember that dry cleaning is more expensive and that it takes longer than laundering.

Just the other day we realized we had given away all of Anna's good dresses, since she now wears only pantsuits or house dresses. We also realized that we do not now have a burial dress for her. It isn't ghoulish to suggest that you set aside a favorite dress or suit for those last rites. As a parent's level of disability increases, you will tend to purchase clothing of a more "leisure" nature, although you may want to retain some more "formal" wear for special occasions. Pantsuits with a minimum of buttons, fasteners, or zippers are the most practical items for women. You may want to experiment with Velcro fasteners. Long, warm housecoats are also useful. Washable sweaters will be welcome as well.

Sport shirts and washable slacks are practical for men. Double-knit slacks come in a variety of colors and patterns and are washable, of course. If your father was a dapper dresser, provide a few dress shirts and clip-on ties (either bow or four-in-hand) that your dad might be able to put on by himself. He'll also enjoy a sweater or two.

For additional warmth, consider shawls or ponchos. Lap robes are useful but should be machine washable.

Include purchases of clothing in your family budget. It is also your responsibility to see that clothing is kept in good repair.

Label Personal Items

If your parent lives in a nursing home, all clothing, including socks and stockings, should be marked or labeled. Indelible ink pens may be purchased in variety stores. Quarter-inch white

I tell you who I am as I sit here so still;
As I use at your bidding, as I eat at your will,
I'm a small child often with a father and mother,
Brothers and sisters, who love one another.
A young girl of sixteen, with wings on her feet.
Dreaming that soon now a lover she'll meet;
A bride soon a-twenty, my heart gives a leap,
Remembering the vows that I promised to keep;
At twenty-five now I have young of my own,
Who need me to build a secure, happy home;
A woman of thirty, my young now grow fast,
Bound to each other with ties that should last.
At forty, my young sons have grown and gone,
But my man's beside me to see I don't mourn.
At fifty, once more babies play round my knee,
Again we know children, my loved one and me.
Dark days are upon me, my husband is dead,
I look to the future, I shudder with dread.
For my young are all rearing young of their own,
And I think of the years and the love that I've known.
I'm now an old woman and nature is cruel—
'Tis jest to make old age look like a fool.
The body it crumbles, grace and vigour depart,
There now is a stone where I once had a heart.
But inside this old carcass a young girl still dwells,
And now again my battered heart swells.
I remember the joys, I remember the pain.
And I'm loving and living life over again.
I think of the years all too few gone too fast,
And accept the stark fact that nothing can last.
So open your eyes, nurse, open and see
NOT a crabbit old woman, LOOK closer,
          SEE ME!

11

❖

Nutrition: All of Us Can Eat Better

There was an old man of Tobago,
Who lived on rice, gruel, and sago;
Till, much to his bliss,
His physician said this—
To a leg, sir, of mutton you may go.

—John Marshall (1755-1835)
Anecdotes of Adventures
of Fifteen Gentlemen

Most books on diet or health foods affirm in some way that "you are what you eat." *Live Longer and Better* is such a book, written by physician Robert Clifford Peale, brother of Norman Vincent. The right kinds of food are especially important for people as they grow older.

Essential Nutrition

Professional nutritionists no longer agree on which "basic foods" are, in fact, essential. However, there is widespread agreement that all of us still need to include in our *daily* diet green and yellow vegetables, fruit, milk or milk products, protein, bread and cereals, and some fat in the form of butter or fortified margarine.

The vegetables can be cooked (frozen or canned, but preferably fresh and *steamed* to retain nutritional value) or eaten raw.

Raw cabbage or salad greens are substitutes for citrus fruits.

Milk can be fluid or in the form of cheese or custards.

Protein is available not only in meat but also in poultry, fish, eggs, beans, peas, nuts, and peanut butter. Rice and beans—a South American staple—is a remarkably good source of complete protein (containing all the essential amino acids). Soy products are also high in protein.

Protein builds and repairs body tissues. Protein deficiency in infants produces *kwashiorkor*, a disease that is prevalent in the hunger areas of our world. One of the serious effects of *kwashiorkor* is brain damage. Evidence is mounting that protein deficiency also has a serious effect upon the brains of older people, and that a return to a balanced diet that includes protein can have some restorative effect.

Of course, when we eat more protein than our bodies need, the excess becomes a source of extra calories. Calories are our bodies' source of heat and energy; when those needs are met, leftover calories result in obesity. Our chief sources of calories are carbohydrates and fats. Fats provide more than twice as many calories per gram as carbohydrates. For example, one tablespoon of butter has as many calories (100) as two tablespoons of sugar. Potatoes, bread, beans, and rice are good sources of carbohydrates.

Vitamins and Minerals

We require a balanced diet because we need the proper mix of vitamins and minerals.

Vitamin A helps maintain health of mucous membranes and skin.

The B vitamins are necessary for our nervous systems, for healthy skin and hair, for good digestion, and to help us better utilize carbohydrates and fats. Niacin deficiency (niacin is a B vitamin) is thought to result in poor mental state and poor skin condition.

Vitamin C is essential for normal body growth, but older people need it, too, for upkeep of bones and teeth. Many people believe this vitamin helps prevent colds.

Vitamin D also promotes growth and assists in absorption of phosphorus and calcium for bones and teeth. Except for those who cannot tolerate milk, the dairy industry's slogan is correct: "You never outgrow your need for milk."

Iron is the blood builder.

And we need iodine for normal function of the thyroid.

Irregularity and Nutrition

According to advertisers, most elderly persons suffer from constipation or irregularity.

The medical advice I've received from our doctors is not to become overly anxious if an older patient doesn't have a daily bowel movement. In fact, don't worry if bowel movements aren't any more frequent than every three days, as long as your parent is eating a well-balanced diet, with raw fruits and vegetables. Include bran and that old standby, prunes or prune juice. Some people find that a daily glass of buttermilk is helpful. Adequate exercise is also beneficial to proper elimination.

If a laxative is necessary, ask your doctor about one of the milder "bulk" preparations such as *Effersyllium* or *Metamucil*. (You may also want to keep a couple of *Fleet* disposable enemas on hand.)

Overnutrition and Undernutrition

As parents of growing children, we learned to prepare foods and monitor eating habits so that essential dietary and nutritional requirements were met.

Younger children are often enticed to eat sweet cereals or snacks. Many teen-agers are undernourished due to their diet of French fries, hamburgers, pizza, and soft drinks. Obesity is sometimes attributed to "overnutrition"—eating too much of the wrong kinds of food.

Our aging parents may not exercise their best judgment where eating is concerned, either. They may rely too much upon a breakfast cereal or an occasional TV dinner, if they live at home. Preparing their own food may seem to be "too much bother." Institutional food may be unpalatable and unchewable.

Some Questions for Dieticians

Institutional meals have been widely criticized—especially in hospitals, but also in nursing homes. There is much blandness, overcooking, and little use of natural foods. Now that microwave ovens are making their appearances in hospitals—sometimes on every wing of every floor—we'll likely see more of the prepack-aged, hastily heated meal. (The same goes for home cooking!)

I am often distressed that institutions providing health care seem to be so little concerned with the food that is cooked and served to patients. I know that many good, qualified people serve as nutritionists and staff dieticians, but I will wager that the nutritional and culinary state-of-the-art in hospitals and nursing homes is far behind intercoms or labs or intensive-care units.

I'm distressed enough to want to ask a few questions, keeping in mind that many private homes need the same admonitions.

Why is so much white bread served? Older people enjoy eating bread, so let's give them whole wheat bread (preferably stone ground). This is one way to provide more nutrients and fiber. And why couldn't institutions bake their own bread, rolls, and muffins on the premises? The smell of baking would certainly be an improvement over some other odors in nursing homes.

Why not provide healthy snack foods? I'd like to see a lot more fresh fruit in hospitals and nursing homes. Some elderly people could not easily handle some fruit; perhaps apples might be cut into quarters and peeled. But most elderly people can manage bananas, tangerines, grapes, plums, and peaches. Most would have no difficulty with carrot sticks, or tiny stalks of celery, or pieces of raw cauliflower and zucchini squash. Such fruits and vegetables might cut down on the desire for sugar, which would be a good thing for older people since they have an increased risk of developing diabetes.

Fruit juice and fruit punch would satisfy the craving for some-thing sweet, provide some vitamins, and enhance kidney func-tion. And fruit juice would be much better than that ubiquitous and dangerous pot of coffee.

While I am mentioning snacks, I would like to propose that all vending machines be banned from patient quarters and areas. Sick and convalescing people do not need the junk food and the soft drinks vending machines dispense. Perhaps the machines could be modified to sell nuts or raisins or dried bananas. Oth-erwise, if vending machines must be kept, place them in staff lounges (although this wouldn't help those staff who need to begin their own weight-control program).

Couldn't cottage cheese and yogurt be used more?

How about hot cereals for breakfast—and grains such as millet and barley and brown rice for other meals, instead of the usual dehydrated potatoes?

There are nutritional advantages in steam-cooking vegetables. But Chinese-type cooking is beneficial in other ways. Stir-frying "extends" meat, doesn't cook vegetables to death, and the smaller pieces of food are easier for older people to eat.

Meat doesn't always have to be served as chopped hamburger. Fish may soon become a luxury food because of its cost, but perhaps small servings of broiled turbot or some other less expensive fish might be served. The price of chicken is always reasonable, and there are many ways to serve it besides frying it. Tasty meat substitutes such as soy products can be used alone in casseroles or as meat extenders. An omelet would be nice now and then.

Why not ban deep-frying? It doesn't help digestion or the cholesterol count.

Liver is a good source of iron and vitamin A. Why must it always be served in fried, leathery form? Most people don't especially like liver, so it has to be made tasty. There are enough recipes—some of them delicious Italian ones—to prepare and disguise liver in new ways.

Casseroles are one way to do this. Why aren't more casseroles prepared in hospitals and nursing homes? This is a great way to combine several dietary essentials in a flavorful, convenient form.

Why not substitute honey for sugar? White sugar is a highly processed food and has no nutritive value. Brown sugar would be a little better, if it isn't artificially colored. Honey contains a few minerals and is a more potent sweetener.

The Value of Good Nutrition

Of course, some of these ideas appear to be costly. Honey is more expensive than white sugar. Perhaps more staff time would be needed for baking, or preparing carrot sticks, or making casseroles. It might require more fuel to cook buckwheat than to make mashed potatoes from a dehydrated mix.

But what would it matter if food and food preparation would

cost more? *Food is part of health care!* The daily charges in hospitals and nursing homes are shockingly high. In the case of hospitals, in addition to subsidizing new equipment and construction, perhaps the time has come to insist that a greater percentage of our health-care dollar go into the right kind of food, properly prepared.

New cooking techniques would have to be learned, but there is evidence that kitchen staffs welcome the opportunity to learn and to be innovative, particularly when they understand the reasons behind better nutrition in the meals they prepare. (The Meadowbrook Hospital in New Orleans offers such evidence.) Food processors, industrial mixers, steamers, and ovens aren't all that expensive, and they cut down on food preparation time. Much could be done, I suspect, with equipment already in hand.

Food Can Be Appetizing

There are a few elderly people who never seem satisfied with the food they are served—or who simply do not have much of an appetite. Making food attractive by awareness of color and use of condiments may help whet jaded or frustrated appetites. I have seen many excellent and attractive meals served in nursing homes. I have also witnessed strange, colorless combinations of purees that turned my stomach.

Anna doesn't use a fork or spoon much anymore. Mostly, she uses her fingers. I try to help her to use the utensils, but perhaps that isn't as important as it once was. However, people like Anna may need to have balanced meals that could be eaten by hand with a minimum of messiness. I think it could be done. Small chunks of meat or fish, without sauce or gravy, some small boiled potatoes or beets, cooked carrots, and some apple slices is the kind of meal I have in mind for Anna and others like her.

Paul has a good appetite and eats everything except pork. We've just found a small plastic device called a "food bumper" that attaches to his plate; it allows him to more easily spoon up his food with his one good hand. Paul has been careful about his food all of his life, and he is a healthier man for it. However, he was selective when he ate away from home, and most of the time someone else prepared his food for him. I sometimes wonder how he would have fared nutritionally had he lived independently for a long period of time.

Leftovers Don't Help

People who live alone often do not eat properly. They tend to snack rather than eat. They often don't bother to cook food, or they rely on simple prepackaged foods. For example, Anna subsisted for too many of her independent years on hot tea and raisin bread.

Dr. Jurgen Schmandt, a political scientist/nutritionist at the University of Texas, believes that older people should never keep leftovers. He feels that too often leftovers become the basis for the next meal or even the next several meals. They are probably eaten cold and do not provide a truly balanced meal. Dr. Schmandt is experimenting with some of the space-age foods developed by N.A.S.A. as possible sources of nutritionally balanced meals for oldsters. Thus far, costs are prohibitive, but these foods offer variety and nutrition and don't have to be heated or cooked.

In the meantime, check on meal habits of parents who live independently.

Had Paul not had his stroke, and were he living close to us, I think Carolyn and I would have tried to provide our own version of balanced "TV dinners." These would have been single portions of foods he liked and needed, made in quantity, frozen, and delivered to him weekly. Paul easily could have managed heating one meal a day.

We probably still would have wanted to check his refrigerator from time to time, just to be sure there were no leftovers or other items waiting to spoil or to become the inadequate makings of future meals. We would want to see that Paul had enough milk, juice, one-serving cans of soup, breakfast cereal, and healthy snacks such as nuts or raisins or other dried fruit.

The kind of monitoring I've described would have been impossible with Paul in Florida and us in Texas. Of course, this was the actuality prior to his stroke, in between his trips to Ecuador. In hindsight, we wish we had done more. We could have arranged with a friend in Florida to look in on Paul and his refrigerator, perhaps doing some of the things we would have done in person. We might have been able to enroll him in either a delivered-meal ("meals-on-wheels") or a congregate-meal ("meals-on-heels") program.

Hints for Jaded Appetites

Each of us has experienced days when even the thought of food wasn't appealing. There are many such days for the elderly, but there are also many nutritious ways to reactivate and excite their appetites.

Our 1946 edition of Irma Rombauer's classic *The Joy of Cooking* included a small section titled "Invalid or Convalescent Cookery." I understand that more recent editions have deleted this valuable section.

Here are just a few items from her list. (The food ought to appeal to tired appetites and should be easy to chew and digest.)

There are dozens of soups and soufflés. Broths, bouillons, cream soups, minestrone, borscht (beet soup), and Swedish fruit soups are just a few of the soup possibilities.

Soufflés can be prepared with strained vegetables, chicken, mushrooms, or cheese. A *timbale* is a "first cousin to the reliable custard and the flighty soufflé," according to Mrs. Rombauer. Actually, the timbale is a kind of custard prepared in individual molds and served with vegetables and a sauce.

Of course, custards are good in their own right. So are puddings and omelets. Flavored gelatin prepared imaginatively is still pleasing.

How about stews that can be eaten with a spoon? There's chicken stew (perhaps with dumplings), oyster stew, beef stew, and lamb stew. Meat pies (or chicken or turkey) offer some of the same possibilities. *Joy of Cooking* includes a recipe for a corn-meal mush meat pie; creamed chicken could be substituted for the meat. This is similar to the various kinds of shepherd's pies.

Better Food for Public Places, by Anne Moyer, emphasizes nutrition and natural foods. Recipes for six "complete protein meatless casseroles" are given. It also offers recipes for ham and bean soup, beef barley soup, cabbage soup, corn chicken soup, lentil soup, and potato soup. Some suggested salads are egg, tuna, ham, curried chicken, or pineapple chicken—all of which include raw vegetables and nuts. More use can be made of sprouts and tofu (soybean curd—there's a recipe for tofu croquettes). Meat loaf can be prepared with oatmeal. Tomatoes can be broiled. There's a good recipe for eggplant parmesan, and much more.

There are many, many possibilities for serving nutritious, tasty, and economical food. What is required is a bit of imagination, planning, and preparation. Surely the benefits to each of us are worth the extra effort.

Resources—Chapter 11

● In your menu planning, you might want to consult such books as *Cooking With Conscience,* by Alice Benjamin and Harriett Corrigan (Noroton, Conn.: Vineyard Books, 1975), *Diet For A Small Planet,* by Frances Moore Lappé (New York: Ballantine Books, 1971), and *More-with-Less Cookbook,* by Doris Janzen Longacre (Scottdale, Penn.: Herald Press, 1976). These books advocate a simplified life-style, and all contain delicious and nutritious recipes that Anna and Paul have enjoyed.

● If you're interested in a career in institutional food service, consult Purdue University (West Lafayette, Indiana 47907) about its *Restaurant, Hotel, and Institutional Management Institute.*

● *Metropolitan Life* offers free booklets on nutrition.

Bogert, L. J., G. M. Briggs, and D. H. Calloway. *Nutrition and Physical Fitness.* Philadelphia: W. B. Saunders, 1973.

Moyer, Anne. *Better Food for Public Places.* Emmaus, Penn.: Rodale Press, 1977.

Natow, Annette B., and Jo-Ann Heslin. *Geriatric Nutrition.* Boston: CBI Publishing Co., 1980.

Peale, Robert Clifford. *Live Longer and Better.* Englewood Cliffs, N. J.: Prentice-Hall, 1961.

12

You Never Outgrow Your Need To Exercise

I get my exercise acting as a pallbearer for my friends who exercise.
—Chauncey Depew (1834-1928),
who, obviously, lived to be
ninety-four.

Despite Mr. Depew's conviction and experience, one of the sad byproducts of our sedentary existence is loss of muscle tone and, thus, loss of energy. Those of us who are desk-bound know the feeling and can more easily recognize what is happening to our handicapped loved ones. For them, unfortunately, lack of exercise often results in a literal atrophy of limbs and muscles.

Exercise is essential for all of us. Although the bedridden are limited by what they can do, even they can benefit from some simple exercises that can be performed in bed.

Walking

For most seniors, walking is still viable and one of the best ways of keeping fit.

Unfortunately, since Anna fell and broke her hip, she no longer walks. Following the operation, she did walk for some three months. Thirty feet with a walker was about all she could manage, but she covered that distance several times a day. The dining room was close to her room and she was able to walk to it. Because of Anna's disorientation, her doctors did not feel physical therapy would be helpful. Then she transferred to another nursing home, and the dining room was a hundred feet or more from her room. She could not manage that great a distance at one time. Since this nursing home did not have enough wheelchairs to transport all of its patients, we purchased a wheelchair for Anna. Our intent was good, but now I think the purchase was a mistake. Anna seems welded to that chair, and she no longer walks.

However, in her own way Anna still gets her exercise. Happily, she is not bedridden. She propels herself with her feet; mostly, she pushes herself backwards (and you had best get out of the way!).

Paul does walk—not quickly nor easily, but he walks. Physical therapy helped him to achieve a measure of mobility, and he retained enough of that instruction to be able to continue to walk, although he still tends to look at his feet when he ought to be looking ahead. Paul does require assistance; he needs someone with a steady grip on his belt and shoulder to aid his sense of balance. He uses a walker—a large four-pronged device that he holds with his left hand—to give him additional stability.

When Paul lived with us, he and Juanita (or Carolyn or myself) walked around our back yard. He still does this when he visits us. When it was raining, he walked down our hallway or along a covered area outside our front door, or on the covered patio in back. Sometimes he would agree to walk the distance of two houses along our street.

There are many places for brief but pleasant walks, indoors and outdoors. Take advantage of these opportunities. We walk with Paul almost every time we visit him at the Trinity Home. There are long wide hallways to use if the weather is inclement, but we much prefer walking outdoors. There is a circle sidewalk, set within a tree-studded court with several handy benches.

If you don't find places to walk, some sort of inexpensive treadmill with sturdy side rails could be purchased or rented. It could be set up in a bedroom, a den, or in the garage.

Establish a routine of walking; keeping to that routine will assist digestion and elimination. It will get the blood flowing back toward the heart. For the elderly, walking is better and safer than jogging, although you'll see the marvelous exceptions in every marathon race.

Like Paul, many older people need assistance as they walk. Don't overprotect, but practice "safety first." Be available if you're needed. Decide how you can keep an older person with more fragile bones from falling.

If your parent receives physical therapy, ask the therapist to teach you the rudiments of "gait assistance"—walking with a handicapped person. Practice with the therapist's supervision. You'll build confidence and develop a new skill. Your walking will be more slowly paced, but that gives you time to chat and observe things as you walk. The time spent walking with a parent can become the best part of a visit.

Cycling

This is a way many older people continue to get their exercise. Of course, it's more practical for those who cycled in their youth and continued the habit during their maturing years. Perhaps you could bicycle together, selecting routes that are reasonably level and safe.

When the weather is bad, an exercycle might be an option. Adapter accessories can convert an ordinary bicycle into a stationary, safe exercycle without the expense of having to buy the real thing.

Large adult-sized tricycles (sometimes called "tri-wheelers") are coming into vogue and are common in many retirement villages. Anyone with the use of arms and legs can ride one, since balance isn't required. Depending upon the amount of traffic, they are reasonably safe. Large wire baskets provide a kind of "trunk" where groceries or plants or packages may be transported. These adult tricycles cost between three hundred and five hundred dollars, and are a practical substitute for automobiles in a neighborhood setting. They are not for busy thoroughfares, but where they can be used they save fuel and hearts.

Other Sports

Swimming and tennis are strenuous and exhausting sports, and should be initiated or continued only with medical approval, providing older persons have built up resistance and stamina over a period of years of consistent involvement with these or similar sports. One generally should not take up tennis at sixty-five, for example; golf might be a better choice.

Swimming is good exercise and has therapeutic value. Special classes to teach the handicapped to swim—or to teach new techniques of swimming—are available in many larger cities. Consult city recreation departments or your local Heart Association for information. Because specially designed facilities and individual instruction are required, costs are sometimes high.

One does not have to aim for changing the record books, although Dr. James Counsilman, swimming coach at Indiana University, did swim the English Channel at fifty-eight. He is the oldest person to have accomplished this feat. Dr. Counsilman is a professional swimmer, has coached several Olympic gold medalists, and proves that with vigorous participation a sport can be continued into more mature years to the point of great endurance.

For most of us, however, swimming is simply a healthy way to relax and strengthen muscles, including the heart, and to relieve the discomfort of back ailments and swollen joints.

Golf also involves many muscles through walking, bending, pulling, and swinging. It also provides the additional benefits of fresh air and sun.

Most team sports are probably too physically demanding for older persons. However, those who were active in softball, basketball, or volleyball might be able to manage some continuing but more restricted involvement.

Some of us have too quickly dismissed *horseshoes* and *shuffleboard* with a condescending smile. A few older people dismiss these as well, seeing them as images of insipid retirement. But both can provide healthy exercise as well as socialization and fun.

Badminton, croquet, and *ping-pong (table tennis)* are other physical activities to consider.

The point is this: As long as we are able, it is more blessed to get off our backsides and to exercise muscles and stimulate the circulation of blood in whatever ways are appropriate and possible, than to be bedridden and allow our muscles to atrophy.

Group Exercise

Dr. Garland O'Quinn, formerly a professor of physical education at the University of Texas in Austin and an Olympic medalist in gymnastics, is now a leader and consultant in developing exercise programs for handicapped persons of all ages. He emphasizes that the purpose of exercise for older people isn't necessarily to exercise but to get people to feel good about themselves and to be happy. Thus, Dr. O'Quinn is cautious about prescribing a rigid physical activity plan for anyone.

However, he cites at least three benefits that result from limited and somewhat structured group exercise.

1) *Music usually accompanies group exercise.* Hearing and reacting to the music is in itself beneficial, says O'Quinn. Furthermore, the rhythm helps pace the group and there is less physical strain.

Children's activities records are sometimes adaptable for this purpose. One is called *Get Fit While You Sit* (released by Educational Activities, Inc., and available through most record stores).

2) *People can learn to maintain and enjoy the physical abilities they still have.* Group exercise for older citizens is not intended to train persons for the Olympics, but such activity can increase a healthy awareness and respect for one's body.

3) *Group exercise, no matter how minimal, will get the blood moving.* The heart pumps blood to our extremities, but the job of helping the heart to pump it back belongs to our muscles. Another physiological benefit of exercise is that more oxygen will get to the lungs. The body will be healthier because of exercise.

When you have opportunity to encourage and lead exercise programs in rest homes or nursing homes, Dr. O'Quinn cautions that you not insist upon total participation. You're not running a military physical fitness program; participation should be an individual decision. People will vary from day to day in their desire to participate and share. They may not feel well, or a gloomy day may induce a gloomy spirit. Observing others can be a mood-lifter, along with tapping toes or fingers to the music or sharing in the laughter.

The following are some simple exercises that can be used:

Squeezing a ball. Use a reasonably hard ball, softball size, or make your own out of cloth and stuffed nylon stockings. Those who have the use of both hands can squeeze or push the ball with both hands.

Persons who are paralyzed can sometimes develop finger

muscles by squeezing or kneading a plastic compound available from durable medical equipment stores or some pharmacies.

Throwing a ball is good exercise; it can even be attempted by someone with a paralyzed hand or arm. Raising the arm and "throwing" the ball (a soft one, like a cloth or sponge rubber ball) even a few inches will be an achievement and will exercise some unused muscles.

Many nursing homes play a kind of circular "kickball." Patients sit in a circle and use hands, not feet, to throw a large beach ball or similar size rubber ball (a medicine ball would be too heavy).

Pulling a rubber band. Obtain a heavy-duty rubber band or cut a strip from an old inner tube. Encourage the patient to stretch the rubber band between two hands. This strengthens reciprocal muscles.

Stand-ups. Simply rising from a chair to a standing position and sitting down again is a helpful and sometimes notable achievement for many older people. The activity is enhanced by making it a rhythmic routine. Cadence count, preferably to music; count to four to stand, four to sit. Repeat ten or twelve times. For persons with leg disabilities or loss of balance, it's helpful to have chairs with armrests so the person has something to push up against. They also ought to have a companion close by to give assistance, if needed. This exercise is a far cry from a regular pushup, but the principle is the same.

Resistance exercise. A partner is needed for this isometric exercise. Both partners either stand or sit facing each other. One person makes fists with both hands, while the partner encloses these with open hands. One pushes outward with his fists while the other pushes inward with his open palms for no more than three or four seconds. (Dr. O'Quinn cautions that it is very important not to carry this exercise to the point of strain.) Or one person can push downward while the other pushes upward. Partners exchange "roles" and direction of pressure. The procedure is to count to four and alternate.

Moving arms and shoulders. You can establish a simple routine of rhythmic calisthenics, whether seated or standing. (1) Extend your arms in front of you; (2) place at your sides; (3) to your knees; (4) at your sides; (5) extend arms above you; (6) again at your sides; (7) twist torso to left, moving arms; (8) then twist

torso to the right, moving arms. Count to eight as you demonstrate this exercise and continue to cadence count as the group
follows your actions. Repeat four or five times. This is a simple
exercise, but it really gets the circulation going.

Moving legs and feet. This exercise should be done while seated.
Establish a rhythmic count. Begin by extending both legs. Raise
the right leg and put it down. Raise the left leg and put it down.
Raise both legs and put them down (this is hard to do; participants may need to push down on the seats of their chairs to do
this part). This exercise can be done to the count of twelve, giving
two counts or beats to each movement.

Here's another way to exercise legs and feet. With the legs
extended, turn or twist feet so the toes touch, then turn or twist
feet so the heels touch. Repeat a dozen times, to music.

Body Movements

There are many simple warm-up exercises that are fun to do
and that are good preparation for more serious exercise. It's
recommended that music be used in warming up as well as in
regular exercising.

I've noticed that even seriously disoriented people enjoy clapping. Begin by counting to the rhythm, then switch to clapping
hands and then hitting knees. Instead of clapping, try flapping
elbows up and down, in cadence!

An alternative to clapping is to hit the palm of the left hand
eight times with the fist of the right hand; then reverse the
activity. Provide scarves or handkerchiefs that can be waved in
a circle, as though preparing to lasso an animal; this is lots of
fun, especially if the scarves are colored—and it gets some neck
and upper back muscles into motion.

If you're playing a march, let the people march. If they have
difficulty walking, they can "march" where they are seated by
raising one foot and then the other. Or you can have them wiggle
their toes or touch toes and heels with each foot, all in cadence.

You might even want to try some "dancing"—which for our
purposes here is merely a euphemism for structured warm-up
exercises.

Contemporary dancing isn't all that complicated, and if your participants can walk, they'll manage a few simple steps. You can create a "disco" by having them take four steps forward and four steps back, twisting hips and swinging arms at will, repeating the action as long as you or your group wish to continue.

Here's another suggestion about music. Choose something with a 4/4 beat, such as "I'd Like To Teach the World To Sing" or "Raindrops Keep Falling on My Head" or a Sousa march. It can be helpful to record the music on a cassette tape. If you can't find music, then cadence count.

A similar program to Garland O'Quinn's is a physical fitness program called *Preventicare,* developed in West Virginia by Lawrence J. Frankel, a physical therapist.

He believes that exercises not only prevent poor circulation, but can help aching joints and muscles, arthritis, and improve coordination and lessen chronic fatigue.

There are fifty *Preventicare* exercises that can be performed in any position a person finds most comfortable—sitting (even in a wheelchair), standing, or lying on the floor or in bed.

Once learned, the exercises can be done by individuals or by groups, without a "professional" on hand to supervise. Mr. Frankel concurs with Dr. O'Quinn in recommending the use of music to establish the pace. He believes the pulse of an older person should not be faster than 120 beats per minute, and music helps control the pulse rate.

Here is a sampling of his exercises.

(1) Tilt your head backward as far as possible, and then forward as far as possible. Do this ten times.

(2) Spread or stretch your fingers on both hands and bring them together repeatedly.

(3) Crumple a page of a newspaper into a ball, using the first joint of each finger, not the palm. Use one hand at a time.

(4) With both hands, push a piece of broomstick (or a large dowel) away from you, then pull it back to your chest.

(5) Stretch out your legs and cross them, right leg over left, then left over right.

Most of these exercises conclude with the instruction, "Continue as long as you can."

That, of course, is good advice for all of us.

Resources—Chapter 12

• You'll find the addresses of Dr. O'Quinn and *Preventicare* in the back of this book.

• In addition to the records referred to in this chapter, you might look for other children's activities records, marching band records, and square dance records. Some of these might be helpful in your own program.

• Check durable medical supply stores and sports equipment stores for items that might be helpful in strengthening unused or weakening muscles. Hand grips, elastic pulls, and plastic substances that can be kneaded (such as *Thera-Plast*) may be useful.

13

Activities Are More Than Busy Work

No, you never get any fun
Out of things you haven't done.
—Ogden Nash (1902-1971)
Portrait of the Artist
as a Prematurely Old Man

How to fill the hours and days of parents who are no longer able to live independently becomes a very large problem for us "caretakers."

Carolyn and I have always rebelled against any form of "busy work" for ourselves, for our children, and more recently for our parents. However, we learned that our parents need ways to occupy their minds as well as their time. We wanted these to be *creative* ways, but we came to recognize that for our parents there was a place for wholesome "busy work."

In this chapter I'm merely going to review some of the things we did. The ideas aren't necessarily original or novel, nor did everything work with equal success.

Books

Be grateful if your parent can still read and likes to read. Books have always been creative ways to deal with isolation and depression, as well as with curiosity.

Get to know the people who staff your local library. Carolyn is a librarian, so Paul and Anna had a friend looking for new books to challenge them. Secure a library card if you don't have one. Libraries lend not only books, but records and tapes and even large framed prints.

Libraries have hundreds of books of all categories printed in large type, which may be easier for your parent to read. The *Reader's Digest* and *The New York Times Magazine* have large-print editions. The *Reader's Digest* also publishes a quarterly book in large print, containing one book condensation and several articles. Perhaps your denomination publishes a magazine for those whose eyesight is failing; many also have more conventional publications for their older members.

Many older people are fascinated by large picture books dealing with travel or nature. If they've done much traveling during their lifetime, they may enjoy remembering those distant places by perusing a good atlas. The *National Geographic* is always pleasant to look at, no matter how ancient the issue.

Identify the books in your parent's own library that were favorites. If the type is too small for your parent to read, read it aloud or give this opportunity to one of your children or a visitor. Perhaps your parent will like to have a favorite volume around just to touch and leaf through.

Recordings

When eyes fail or simply don't make out the words because of brain damage, having someone else read a book is a way to keep up with life and ideas.

You will want to do some of this yourself. There is much satisfaction in reading aloud to someone else—and our busy lives too often deny us this privilege. You may want to record some of this reading, so your parent could listen while you are occupied elsewhere.

However, it is also good to remember that there are many services ready for your call.

In many areas, National Public Radio broadcasts "From the Bookshelf" five days a week, an excellent way to "read" current bestsellers.

State libraries have large sections devoted to materials for the blind and visually handicapped. Thousands of books have been recorded on cassette tapes, and the federal government provides free postage to and from the library. The Library of Congress provides a free cassette player to play these tapes. Check with your state commission for the blind or with your library for more information. Medical certification of need may be requested.

The Jewish Guild for the Blind specializes in recording current bestsellers, both fiction and nonfiction. Professional narrators or actors read the books, and sound effects are sometimes incorporated to make the book come more "alive." (The society's address is listed in this chapter's "Resources.")

Various Christian organizations provide devotional and Bible study materials on cassette tape. Some are loaned; others must be purchased. Several versions of the Scriptures have been recorded. I have a special fondness for the version distributed by the American Bible Society, narrated by Alexander Scourby. The *Unshackled!* dramatic radio series is now available for home listening. The Reigner Library of Union Theological Seminary (Richmond, Virginia) has the most extensive listing of lectures and Bible studies in the country. Check this chapter's "Resources" for other ideas and sources.

If your parent enjoys music, records can be borrowed from your library or from friends. Portable record players are often loaned as well, but these are rarely of the high-fidelity type. You might want to have favorite music recorded onto cassette tape, as cassette players are much simpler for handicapped persons to use.

Volunteer Work

As long as your parent is able and willing, collaborate with agencies seeking volunteer help. The wisdom and expertise of elderly people is a vast, untapped resource in many fields.

Foster grandparents are needed in homes for the mentally retarded. Sitters are welcomed in day-care centers and church nurseries (churches sometimes pay a nominal stipend for this service). Volunteers are needed in nursing homes to write letters, read letters, help patients with shopping, arrange for parties, or just to be a friend to someone who doesn't have one.

Coordination of such volunteer opportunities is often done by RSVP—the *Retired Senior Volunteer Program,* funded through Vista—usually listed in the telephone directory.

SCORE—*Service Corps of Retired Executives*—is an organization that provides free management counseling to small businessmen and community groups. For information, consult your local office of the Small Business Administration.

Many cities have an Adult Services Council that provides information on services and opportunities for older adults. Check the telephone book, your local library, your local chapter of the AARP (American Association of Retired Persons), or your local welfare or human resources agency.

Crafts

A parent who likes to sew, crochet, embroider, and knit will likely want to continue. Anna enjoyed embroidery for several years. There are two quilting groups in Paul's nursing home; one is for the "perfectionists" and the other is for those who are interested but whose attention to detail is waning.

You will want to make sure projects are manageable. This may mean finding smaller pieces to embroider with simpler designs or providing a larger set of needles for making a larger-than-normal afghan. Your parent might like to learn new skills in needlepoint or similar crafts. New materials and techniques are constantly coming along; you might want to visit a craft shop every few months just to browse and get ideas.

If men enjoy woodworking and are still able to use tools, this may be the opportunity to make that dollhouse for a great-grand-daughter or a rocking horse for a great-grandson. If they are into electronics, this might be the time to get into ham radio or making a mini-computer.

Leathercraft and ceramics may be crafts that could be continued. Using one's skills in crafts is a fine way to make gifts for the family or to earn some extra money.

We are extremely fortunate to have a parks and recreation department in Austin that gives serious attention to the needs of senior citizens. It operates several day activity centers. It also provides an opportunity for displaying and selling crafts in an annual fair at the Municipal Auditorium and in a store, open throughout the year and located on "Main Street" in Austin. The store is in a building called *The Bakery* (built by Swedish immigrants) and is an official historical monument. The wares are varied and exquisite (such as delicately painted porcelain). Many frontier skills are being preserved, and many people are productively happy.

Hobbies

Hobbies are a bit difficult to begin in later life, but unlike taking up a strenuous sport, it is possible.

Perhaps your parent had some interest for which he or she never felt there was time; now there is time to explore, to learn, and to enjoy. If your parent had the foresight to initiate a hobby, that interest can be cultivated and continued now.

Many older people discover enjoyment in painting. Anna Mary Robertson Moses, better known as "Grandma Moses," began her new career in her seventies.

Paul has come to enjoy coloring pictures. We first supplied him with paint-by-number books that required watercolors. It was a challenge to keep the brush within the lines with his left hand, but he improved. We found posters that he colored with felt pens, and he completed these as gifts for his grandchildren. We found pictures on which pigment was already printed; they only required a wet brush. But the colors were not vivid and the pictures weren't much of a challenge.

Most recently, Carolyn found a nice collection of birds to color, and Paul is extremely proud of his work with these. Carolyn placed some Audubon prints around his room to inspire him. He's using something called a *crapon*; it looks like a crayon but isn't waxy. It isn't chalk, but it is a kind of pastel that has vivid colors and can be rubbed with interesting effect.

Bellerophon Books and Dover Publications publish a variety of coloring books, many of which are really for adults. History, art, nostalgia, and nature are some of the subjects. Concordia publishes oversized coloring posters. Check your bookstore or write to us for information.

Shop art supply stores just as you would craft and hobby shops for new ways for handicapped persons to use color. There are many varieties of colored pencils. There is charcoal and chalk. There are chalk-type materials that can be rubbed onto a picture and then painted with a wet brush.

Your parent's dexterity, muscle coordination, ability to grip and grasp, and eyesight will determine what kinds of materials are most suitable.

If your parent's hobby was photography, perhaps this could

be continued. Provide film for pictures or slides. Help your parent to consolidate and catalog the results of this lifetime hobby. Make copies of prized pictures for grandchildren. Make scrapbooks.

Collecting stamps and coins may require a strong magnifying glass, but these hobbies appreciate in value and interest. Borrow the latest stamp and coin catalogs from your library. Additions to the collection make good gifts.

Perhaps your parent collected stones but never had time to polish them. Now is the time to obtain a tumbler. This won't require much physical exertion, but the process will be fascinating. A spin-off might be some jewelry-making.

Back to Nature

Gardening and bird-watching are hobbies many older people find they can continue to enjoy.

About ten years ago we purchased a canary for Anna. She enjoyed his singing, and she followed the book in caring for her "Georgie."

For Paul's most recent birthday we decided to give him a bird bath and feeder, placed just outside his window. We keep the feeder supplied weekly with seed, and we clean the bath and fill it with fresh water; some friends we've met also help keep the bath operational. Paul delights in watching the antics of his feathered friends. There are the usual sparrow hangers-on, but there are also a pair of mockingbirds, some cardinals, and several boisterous and messy blue jays. The birds bring enjoyment to several other residents who see them through their windows as well.

When Paul lived with us, we encouraged his interest in plants by providing him with his own miniature "garden plot"—a six-foot-long window box placed on bricks so it was within his reach. He planted lettuce and radishes in summer. Later in the year he planted flowers. He enjoyed both watching the growth and participating in the harvest. This was the only part of our garden that received a superabundance of water, as Paul insisted on watering his garden every day.

One of Paul's friends sent him an amaryllis plant a couple of years ago. It arrived early enough to bloom at Eastertime, and it continues to bring enjoyment every spring. Plants require care, but they do make fine gifts.

Games

Anna was the game player in our family. She thoroughly enjoyed checkers, picture and crossword puzzles, *Monopoly,* and *Scrabble.* Back in 1937, we played our way across the Atlantic on an eleven-day freighter voyage to Europe. Just ten years ago, she could whiz through a thousand-piece jigsaw puzzle in a day or two. Sadly, those days are no more.

Paul and Anna both grew up in an environment in which "worldliness" meant playing cards, attending movies, dancing, smoking, and drinking alcoholic beverages. The Sabbath was to be strictly observed as a day of worship and rest. Since so many sports events took place on Sundays, professional sports were ignored and certainly not encouraged.

Anna was not disloyal to her heritage, but she hedged a bit. She made certain that she and I both saw the nature and travel films shown most Saturdays at Chicago's Field Museum. Visiting the Christmas shows in the huge department stores of Chicago's Loop was a highlight every December.

Paul did not hedge. He was never enthusiastic about games, and I'm sure he was often distressed with Carolyn and me for taking him to day activities centers where people actually seemed to be enjoying their card games.

Nevertheless, Paul has begun to make some concessions. Earlier I mentioned his new interests in television, including sports. Occasionally he will tackle a picture puzzle, although the puzzle must be simple and broad in design, with large, easy-to-fit pieces. He has learned to play dominoes and is getting rather good at it.

Games are important as ways to retain mental agility and to bring people of all ages together, especially on a one-to-one basis. Games help to bridge generation gaps, and they help us to enjoy each other's company when conversation wanes or wanders.

On my way to visit Paul at Trinity Home, I often drive past a group of four elderly men seated around a barrel in "downtown" Round Rock. They play dominoes and checkers, and I understand they usually defeat any young challenger.

I used to enjoy watching people play chess on the concrete tables in New York's Washington Square. Many of the players were old-timers and were experts at the game.

However, I can't remember ever seeing anyone playing chess in a nursing home, although I have seen some bridge played. If some people remember the rules of bridge, surely others remember the gambits of chess. Is this absence of chess—if I have observed correctly—due, perhaps, to the fact that we don't usually consider giving games of skill to nursing home residents? I believe that chess, backgammon, and many of the new strategy games would appeal to many older persons.

I recently rediscovered some flash cards that we used for phonics and word association with our three children. I took them with me the next time I visited Anna. Her attention to the cards lasted only about ten minutes, but during that time her interest was keen. She tried to speak some of the words and often came very close to doing so. She identified several numbers. We played with the pictures she especially liked—the sheep, the dog, the little girl with her basket of flowers. I'd put these face down on the table and she would slowly turn them over and smile and sometimes try to say the word. I'm going to keep up this activity, hoping it might help her overcome some of her jargon-speech problem.

If flash cards have a use, then I feel Lotto games of all types would likely be fun for many residents. Other simple games could be tried—games that have movement and an element of competition, but that do not require much abstract reasoning. Games might be a way to enliven your visits with parents. When you find one that really clicks, you might want to leave it at the nursing home for your parent and a friend to play.

Some nursing homes make a special effort to encourage socialization of residents through games and parties. Bingo (without money winners) is a favorite in many homes. Monthly birthday parties are common—all residents who have had a birthday during the month are honored, and all residents are invited. Here is a place where family help and participation is welcomed. Anna's nursing home is now beginning a "happy hour" twice a week from 3:00 to 4:00 P.M., when fruit punch and sandwiches or cookies are served. Records are played and a few body movement exercises are tried, although this is not billed nor planned as an exercise period. Everyone seems to have a better time than usual.

A nursing home up in the hill country of Texas now has a monthly wine and cheese party. I understand that it really *is* a "happy hour"!

Television

Some of us self-appointed intellectuals have frowned upon television and criticized it. I've done my share of pontificating (having worked professionally in television), feeling that its potential is so rarely achieved. I used to think of television as a kind of sedative or an electronic "sitter" for older people.

I'm changing my mind. One must still be selective, as there is a lot of trash on TV. Some of it is fluff, some of it is destructive, and young and old are victimized. But we ought not damn the medium because of its product or the character of those who merchandise froth and filth. There are many good programs on TV, both on educational and commercial networks.

Anna's interest span is now too brief to enjoy television, but she once was an avid fan, just as she was once a consistent reader of serial stories in magazines. Paul long enjoyed the news programs and features on TV, even before his stroke. Today, television is much more a part of his world.

I check the weekly TV schedule and make a chart showing the programs I think Paul will enjoy. On a large sheet of paper, using big letters and numbers, I color code the time and channel (I also circle the channel). I tape this chart to the wall next to his TV set. When there's a program we've missed or something special like a presidential news conference comes on, we call the nurse on duty and ask her to tell Paul and turn on the set or change channels.

Paul has his favorites. He enjoys the continuity and family life of *Little House on the Prairie* and *The Waltons*. He roars at reruns of *I Love Lucy* and *Gilligan's Island*. He's captivated by *Wild Kingdom*, as well as the Cousteau and *National Geographic* specials. He likes some of the *Nova* series on public television; many of the historical series are also important to him. He isn't able to get the Christian Broadcasting Network programs presently, but he has a favorite Sunday church service he watches when he isn't visiting us, and he wants to see every Billy Graham crusade special.

A new cable service will soon reach Paul's nursing home, and his program choices will be greater. He'll be able to include CBN in his viewing, for example. Cable News Network will be another new choice—news twenty-four hours a day if he wants it!

I wish more of us could afford home videocassette recorders. There are many late-evening specials—as well as a few classic motion pictures—that older people never see because they are usually in bed by nine. I'll return to this concern later in discussing some challenges churches and other sponsor groups might explore.

Incidentally, we bought a new TV set for Paul. It's a good *color* set, but more importantly, it has a simple remote device that allows him to change channels and adjust the volume with his good left hand. He can use the remote unit from any part of the room, so it permits him greater control over his viewing.

An aide told me he followed both political conventions in 1980, watching from his bed and staying awake far beyond his usual bedtime.

Radio

The homebound have enjoyed listening to the radio since its earliest days in the 1920s. Despite the abundance of television programming, especially with new cable systems, radio may still be the preferred medium for your parent.

Radio continues to provide news and coverage of special events and sports. FM radio brings music of all types with a minimum of interruption.

Many radio stations target their programming to smaller audiences. Thus, there are twenty-four-hour-a-day news stations, classical music stations, ethnic stations, and Christian stations.

Radio drama is making a comeback. Mystery and adventure have returned to commerical radio. Public radio is dramatizing the classics or experimenting with new dramatic works as in its "Earplay" series.

Public radio, in fact, presents many interesting choices. British and Canadian programs are rebroadcast. Books are read. Special coverage is given to congressional hearings.

Many listeners enjoy the "talk shows"—the interviews and the phone-in questions and responses. Many elderly persons are regular participants in such programs.

Shortwave reception is better than ever—and there is excitement in listening to Hilversum or Moscow or London or Quito.

There are even special radio sets that provide twenty-four-hour weather forecasts. Push a button and you hear your local U.S. Weather Bureau.

Radio may be an ideal companion for your loved one.

Creative Achievements

In looking through a book called *Play Activities for the Retarded Child* (by Bernice Wells Carlson and David R. Ginglend, published by Abingdon), I wondered if there were ideas that might be adapted for people suffering from the classical symptoms of senility, who do not participate in the kinds of games and activities we've been discussing thus far.

The book offers many suggestions for games, handicrafts, and music. Many of the motion songs would be enjoyed by most nursing home residents.

The authors make two points in their discussion of handicraft skills and retarded children that apply to our topic in this chapter.

First, they say it is important for a child to see the results of his efforts. This is especially important to a person who is constantly frustrated. The application for older frustrated persons is that crafts or games or activities must be simple and manageable enough so that some result is visible and achievable. We must not expect too much. We must not do too much. But we can certainly try to provide creative opportunities to overcome frustration and depression.

Secondly, the authors point to the need for a feeling of achievement. "The act of producing something of his own gives a child a feeling of confidence and achievement." Oldsters also face this need. For so many of them, life is programmed and monitored and guided by government regulations or by us; they need opportunities to create, to express themselves, and to produce something tangible that they enjoy and that others may admire.

This is why the city of Austin sponsors an annual fair featuring handicrafts produced by its senior citizens. This is why RSVP holds an annual banquet honoring its senior volunteers, giving them plaques and pins and special recognition. This is why some nursing homes proudly display art work and other crafts made by residents.

And this is why we must keep looking for new ways to dispel frustration and foster confidence and achievement in those we love.

Resources—Chapter 13

● Look for support groups that can help your parent and you. The American Heart Association, for example, sponsors *Stroke Clubs* throughout the nation. Similar groups have been formed for persons coping with cancer or Parkinson's Disease or diabetes.

● Sources for cassette tapes:

Jewish Guild for the Blind, 15 W. 65 St., New York, NY 10023.

Lutheran Tape Ministry, Box 125, Seward, NE 68434. (Offers some material in German.)

Pacific Garden Mission, 646 S. State St., Chicago, IL 60605. (Distributes copies of its *Unshackled!* radio drama series.)

Reigner Recording Library, Union Theological Seminary, Richmond, VA 23227. (This may be the largest religious tape cassette library anywhere. Catalog must be purchased.)

Also, consult your state's Commission for the Blind for Library of Congress taped materials.

● An excellent book is *Activities for the Aged and Infirm,* by Toni Merrill (Springfield, Ill.: Charles C. Thomas, 1977). The book is described as a "handbook for the untrained worker." Now in its sixth printing, it is comprehensive, practical, and packed with ideas and sketches.

● From time to time Carolyn and I plan to offer new activities ideas we discover. If you'd like to be on our mailing list, write the Gillies at 9303 Hunters Trace East, Austin, Texas 78758.

● An activity I didn't discuss in this chapter is continuing education. Many older people want to stretch their minds. Some want to return to college and complete work toward a degree. Universities and colleges often offer noncredit courses for general enrichment of life. Austin provides a variety of educational experiences for adults, held in the afternoons in neighborhood schools after the children have finished their classes. Some examples include lawn mower repair, simple auto mechanics, office skills, foreign languages, folk dancing, and photography.

● An exciting program that combines serious continuing education with travel to major campuses is *Elderhostel*. You must be sixty or older to qualify. More than three hundred colleges and universities are now signed up for this adventure in learning. For information, write Elderhostel, 100 Boylston St., Suite 200, Boston, MA 02116.

● Two good sources for information about volunteer work opportunities are RSVP *(Retired Senior Volunteer Program)*, usually related to the federally funded ACTION program, and SCORE *(Service Corps of Retired Executives)*, supervised by the Small Business Administration. There may be an Adult Services Council in your city that can provide you with additional information about these and other volunteer opportunities. Check the white pages of your telephone book for addresses and telephone numbers.

14

Parenting Where It Often Hurts: Money and the Law

*We get too soon old
and too late smart.*
—Pennsylvania Dutch saying

Responsibility for your aging parent or parents includes financial and legal responsibility.

This is something most of us would rather avoid. We don't want to know about our parents' financial affairs, particularly when they are still living. It seems like meddling or an intrusion.

Parents may also choose to be close-mouthed about their financial resources or condition; often this is due to their desire to hold on to those resources so you and others might benefit after their death. They want enough to live on without being a burden, and they want something left over as a legacy. If you have brothers and sisters or in-laws, the possibility for further misunderstanding always exists where financial matters are concerned. We all know instances where seemingly solid family relationships have been ruptured over money and property.

Nevertheless, when a parent no longer can manage his or her own affairs conveniently and competently, someone has to fill the gap and take charge. That person may be you.

I am not a lawyer and I am not qualified to give legal advice. But I will mention several areas about which I think you should have concern, about which you should seek legal opinion, and about which you should take some action.

Do secure professional guidance. There are books dealing with family law and estate matters that you can borrow from your library. There is an excellent "Consumer Survival Kit" (related to the PBS-TV series) on law called *Advise and Represent*. Last, but by no means least, consult with your own attorney.

Securing a Lawyer

Ask friends or neighbors about lawyers who have helped them, particularly in matters affecting older persons.

Call your local bar association and ask for assistance. Usually you will be given several names.

Consult the Martindale-Hubbell Legal Directory, found in most public libraries. This multi-volume directory lists lawyers by city and state, gives their age, educational background, years of practice, specialties, and a rating. Not every lawyer is rated, and an absence of rating does not mean the lawyer is inexperienced or incompetent. Check the names you have gathered with the directory.

Telephone for an appointment, verifying the cost of a consultation fee. Then discuss your needs (and costs) and decide whether you wish to hire this particular attorney. (If you hire a person and later become dissatisfied with the quality of his work or effort, you also have the right to fire him.)

Medical Benefits

There is a difference between Medicare and Medicaid.

Medicare is the health-care coverage provided to anyone receiving Social Security or railroad retirement benefits. You are automatically eligible at age sixty-five unless you say you don't want it; the Social Security people provide information on how to refuse this medical insurance. Medicare is a shared-cost program. As of July 1, 1980, the monthly premium deducted from Social Security checks was $9.60.

Medicaid is medical insurance for those who don't qualify for Medicare or who can't afford to pay for the Medicare "gaps" (we'll discuss these in a moment). Medicaid is free to people on Supplemental Security Income (SSI) and other public assistance programs. Thus, Medicaid is not limited to people sixty-five or older. In fact, Medicaid provides certain screening exams, and treatment programs for persons under twenty-one, and home health care for eligible persons over twenty-one. Medicaid is financed by federal and state governments and is administered by state welfare agencies. It is available to many persons on welfare; however, it is not limited to such persons, as we shall see.

Back to Medicare.

Medicare is a kind of co-insurance, with deductibles, and its premium cost and benefits change from year to year.

These are the present benefits, as of January 1, 1981.

Upon entering a hospital, you pay $204 (a kind of deductible). For the next sixty days, Medicare pays all your hospital costs. If you don't stay the full sixty days but must reenter the hospital during the calendar year, you do *not* have to pay that $204 a second time. If your hospital stay goes beyond sixty days, you begin to share costs. For the sixty-first through the ninetieth day, you will pay $51 a day; Medicare pays the rest.

"Reserve days" are sometimes needed for extended hospital stays. You are given sixty such days, which you may use at any time during your lifetime. You may use these after you've stayed in a hospital ninety days. For each "reserve day" used, however, you must pay $102, with Medicare paying the rest. (Obviously, one hopes hospital stays will be well under sixty days.) What I've described is the basic hospital benefit under Medicare's "Part A."

"Part B" is called "supplemental medical coverage" and pays for physicians' and surgeons' fees, medical services and supplies, outpatient hospital care, some home health care, and a portion of psychiatric outpatient care. You must pay the first $60 (the deductible) during the calendar year; Medicare then pays 80 percent of the remaining "reasonable" charges (which it determines and establishes). If doctors' fees are higher than the Medicare standard, then you must pay that difference, plus your share (20 percent) of "approved" charges. Medicare pays the full amount of some laboratory fees.

Let me use Paul's experience as an example of how this works out, based on benefits and deductibles applicable in 1976.

Paul spent fifty-eight days in St. Paul-Ramsey Hospital in St. Paul. His total hospital bill was $10,244. Paul was required to pay $140 upon admission (as noted, this required amount is now $204). Medicare paid for all other hospital charges except a wheelchair rental and a small amount ($9.60) for "take-home drugs." Paul's doctors' bills totaled $931, of which Medicare paid only $492.

Medicare pays for some nursing home costs. If your doctor decides you can continue therapy and convalesce in a skilled nursing facility rather than staying on in a hospital, Medicare will pay all the costs for the first twenty days. Thereafter, up to the hundredth day, you will share in the costs by paying $25.50 for each day. You must enter the nursing home from a hospital, so you will already have paid the initial $204. *Medicare pays nothing for nursing home care after the hundredth day,* and it pays only for *skilled* care. (Not every nursing home is licensed to provide Type IV or "skilled" care, nor will every skilled nursing home accept Medicare patients. Paul was classified as Type III, not requiring constant nursing attention. Thus, Medicare paid nothing toward his nursing home costs.)

Medical costs are frightening. I don't know what we would have done without Medicare assistance; we breathed our thanks many times for the 1935 legislation that eventually made Medicare (and Medicaid) possible. As the debate about a national health insurance plan continues, we'll be hearing much more about these kinds of "catastrophic" medical costs.

There are gaps in Medicare—the deductibles and extra charges the patient must pay. Persons eligible for Medicaid are covered for these extra costs. The rest of us must find other ways to meet them.

A "self-insurance" emergency cash fund might be established. However, supplementary health insurance plans that take Medicare into account should be considered. These fill in the gaps; they pay for that initial $204, for the extra hospital room costs after day sixty-one, and they pick up the 20 percent (or more) of physicians' fees and some laboratory fees. Blue Cross/Blue Shield, the American Association of Retired Persons, and other groups offer plans that could be explored. Be wary of mail-order or newspaper-supplement offers. Read the fine print. Some pay nothing for the first week of hospital care. Few provide any nursing-home or psychiatric-care benefits. Nevertheless, good policies are available to help cushion the financial impact upon savings, especially during extended illnesses.

Contact your local Social Security office for information about Medicare. Be sure your parent or parents have a Medicare card, if they are eligible.

Medicaid has already been defined, but let's have a closer look. Many welfare recipients are eligible for Medicaid. Recipients of SSI (Supplemental Security Income), those who receive no or minimal Social Security benefits, are also eligible for Medicaid. SSI payments are presently available to persons receiving $228 or less per month. However, eligibility criteria have been changing annually, and current information should be obtained from your local Social Security office.

You do not have to be on welfare to qualify for Medicaid. You don't have to be on Social Security, either. There are limits, of course—and each state sets its own rules—but people within a range of incomes may receive Medicaid benefits. Those with the lowest incomes get it free; others pay a certain portion. Contact your local public assistance or welfare office for eligibility requirements in your state.

In general, Medicaid picks up where Medicare leaves off; it pays for the deductibles and the shared costs. Medicaid also pays for up to three drug prescriptions per month; for eyeglasses; and for hearing aids. There are other health benefits, such as dental care.

Anna qualifies for and receives Medicaid assistance. Because of this, I no longer carry supplemental health insurance for her. Between Medicare and Medicaid, she has comprehensive health coverage.

In Texas, to be eligible for Medicaid you may own some property (such as a house and a car), and your cash assets must be no more than $1500. Cash assets include checking and savings accounts, securities, and paid-up insurance (which, of course, could be converted into cash). Remember that the criteria vary from state to state.

Anna owns no property. She has long since exhausted her savings. She has some paid-up insurance, but its value is less than $1500. Her Social Security check is presently around $269 per month. I am allowed to retain $25 of this for her personal expenses. This is kept in a separate account. The remainder, approximately $244, is paid monthly to the nursing home, and the State of Texas makes up the difference with Medicaid funds.

The correct way to describe Anna is that she is a "Medicaid recipient"; she is not "on welfare."

However, to arrange for Anna's Medicaid benefits it was necessary to apply through the state welfare department, which, in

Texas, *administers* the program. Once a nursing home was selected, I was assigned to a social worker who provided me with information and forms, which Anna ultimately had to sign (she now signs with a "mark"), with witnesses. I must file new forms every six months.

I understand the relationship with the state agency much better now. However, on my first visit I had deep feelings of guilt and irresponsibility. I was Anna's son; I shouldn't ask the state to support her. But on the other hand, I didn't have the $800 or so, required then, to pay for Anna's *monthly* nursing home charge. Mostly, I was fighting the idea of *my* mother being on welfare. I had to learn that Medicaid is a form of health insurance and not "welfare," as I and so many others understood it.

Furthermore, I had to recognize something about the law. I was caring for Anna, and would continue to assume responsibility for her. But she is a person with her own rights under the law, and she qualifies for certain kinds of assistance. I have helped pay for that assistance over many years as a taxpayer and a contributor to the Social Security system. Someone close to me is now the beneficiary.

Nursing Home Costs

Nursing home costs are climbing, along with everything else. They may be a bit lower in the Southwest, where we live, but at the present time the cost of a semi-private room in this area *begins* at $25 a day. Paul now pays $30 a day (up from $26 a year ago) for a private room, but that is still unusually low because the cost is subsidized in part by the Lutheran Church. Nursing home costs in the Southwest range from $25 to $50 a day. Meals are included, of course. Laundry may be included. Daily rates are 10 to 25 percent higher elsewhere.

When you multiply the daily rate by the number of days in a year, you arrive at an annual expenditure that is shocking.

It may be tempting to consider home care strictly for economic reasons. However, keep in mind that home care involves the employment of extra help, modifications to your home, and higher utility and laundry costs. The cost of institutional care is high, but so is the cost of home care.

The possibility of such heavy expenditure must be faced squarely. Children may have to share in the costs. Parents' savings must be preserved in a way that they will be available but not quickly exhausted. Additional insurance coverage should be sought, including the possibility of Medicaid.

Money Matters

Inflation may have its greatest impact upon the lives of the elderly. It affects their fixed incomes and their savings. Medical health care costs were never higher, and are increasing. The cost of housing is said to be the second greatest problem of the elderly.

As you assume the role of parent, you must evaluate your parent's economic situation, make adjustments and judgments, and do your best to stretch those resources so that adequate care and comfort will be provided. You do this knowing that you will likely have to make up the difference or find some other way to manage when your parent's resources are exhausted. Longevity affects economics, which affects each of us. And it will have a still greater impact upon our children.

I think your chief goal ought to be liquidity. Long-term investments are especially attractive in a time of inflation, but sufficient cash must be available to pay bills.

I maintain a separate checking account and two savings accounts for Paul. (Incidentally, the bank I use makes no charge for senior citizen checking accounts.) One savings account is a regular passbook account; withdrawals can be made at any time. The other account is a six-month certificate-of-deposit (or "money-market") account that earns more interest but doesn't tie up Paul's money for any long period of time. I maintain only a passbook savings account for Anna. Carolyn is cosigner with me for all of these accounts; if anything should happen to me, she could manage these financial affairs of both parents without waiting for a court determination or settlement.

These separate accounts greatly facilitate my bookkeeping. I can easily verify all receipts and expenditures, since all checks and other income sent to Paul or Anna are immediately deposited.

The savings accounts are trust accounts; they bear the Social

Security number of either Paul or Anna. Interest is credited to them, not to me, and is so reported to the Internal Revenue Service.

I want to underscore something about investments.

Paul is not a wealthy man; few missionaries are. His Social Security benefits, a small pension, a continuing small stipend from a supporting church, and interest from investments pays for about 65 percent of his monthly expenses. The remainder comes from his savings, supplemented by the family.

Paul invested in the Lord's work—in the areas of church planting, Bible distribution, and retiree centers through local church programs. He has no commercial or governmental securities. He owns no life insurance, either.

Most of his investments are in bonds, several of which will not mature for five to eight years. They can't be cashed in without substantial loss; thus, they provide limited convertible assets. Two of the three retiree centers Paul invested in have gone bankrupt. Settlement for one was made a few months ago on the basis of slightly less than ninety cents on the dollar; interest for the past several years was lost, in addition to the 10 percent loss on the actual investment. The second bankruptcy is still in litigation.

I have learned from being Paul's trustee that an inexperienced investor like myself should stay with reliable savings institutions that are federally insured.

Legal Instruments

How may the affairs of a disabled or handicapped parent best be handled?

A Trust. A simple trust can be drawn, naming a friend, a family member, or a banking institution as trustee. The trustee's obligations are defined. Property transferred to the trustee is used for the care and protection of the parent. Upon the parent's death, property is distributed as the trust instructs. Regular accounting is required. The trust may be revoked at any time by the parent. A lawyer must be consulted to devise a trust that may require only official recording in the court to become operative.

A trust may be drawn if the parent is lucid and alert and is only physically disabled.

Guardianship. If the parent is mentally incompetent and is unable to designate a trustee, then the court must appoint a guardian or a conservator. This may be someone the family recommends or someone the court feels can serve best in this capacity. A lawyer is needed to advise and draw up the required petition.

Power of Attorney. This is authorization for someone to act on another's behalf. It can grant general or specific authority. A parent may grant general authority to someone to handle all affairs. Or the parent may authorize something specific, such as opening a checking account or selling securities or property.

Some lawyers advise against using power of attorney. They point out that the authorization is valid only as long as the maker is competent. The authorization also ends with the maker's, or grantor's, death.

You can buy standard power-of-attorney forms in a legal stationery store. I did just that before flying up to St. Paul to see Paul after his stroke. I also consulted a couple of family law books as well as my attorney before I left. Since Paul had named me executor of his will, I had some idea of his assets and the scope of what I might have to handle. I took the form with me for Paul to sign.

I discussed it with the hospital business manager, and he discussed it with Paul. The business manager was convinced that Paul understood and agreed with the provisions. He and another person witnessed Paul's "x," and I became Paul's limited agent, his "attorney-in-fact." This allowed me to handle such matters as his banking affairs, cashing his bonds upon maturity, and selling his car.

Although I see the necessity for trusteeships and guardianships, I believe the power of attorney is a valuable and essential first step. Some states allow the possibility of a power of attorney taking effect only with the disability of the "principal"; thus, it can be prepared in advance of any real need. Also, powers of attorney can specify a date when the power will end. If the principal becomes incompetent, some states do allow the power of attorney to continue. Other states make quick provision for temporary guardianship.

Executor. This is the person named in a will to carry out its provisions. If you are named, you are free to serve or to decline. It would be helpful to discuss the matter with the lawyer who drew up the will.

The list of responsibilities of an executor is long, dealing with matters of probate, creditors, taxes, and distribution of assets. Such lists may be available from your library, your lawyer, your insurance agent, or your mortician.

You will also want to check with your local Internal Revenue Service office about required forms and declarations for executors.

Representative Payee. This is a Social Security term describing someone who serves as an agent in receiving and depositing Social Security checks. I've arranged for Paul's check to be deposited directly into his checking account. I receive Anna's check and deposit it in her savings account. As a representative payee, I must keep adequate records of these transactions should the Social Security Administration require verification of any transaction relating to its funds. You can apply for representative payee status at your local Social Security office, where you can also obtain an excellent guide on specific procedures.

Legal Counsel

As you deem appropriate, consult with your attorney about contractual matters, such as an agreement with a nursing home, an insurance policy, a complicated transfer of property, or a careful review of a "life care" retirement center contract.

When issuers of bonds default or declare bankruptcy, you will need legal representation to follow through on the hearings and advise you on the various plans of settlement that may be offered.

If your parent hasn't made a will, bring your parent and a lawyer together for this purpose. Preparing a will is not expensive, and it doesn't have to be complicated. A "letter of instructions" indicating disposition of household effects and other wishes can be stated informally; this does not have to be part of the will.

Wills don't have to be drawn up in a lawyer's office; they are valid if properly witnessed. John B. Kelly, Princess Grace's father, was a maverick millionaire who wrote his own will. He didn't like

legal jargon, asserting that "kids will be 'kids' and not 'issue.'"
He began his will this way: "This is my last will and testament
and I believe I am of sound mind. Some lawyers will question
this when they read my will; however, I have my opinion of some
of them, so that makes us even." His will wasn't questioned, but
personally, I'd rather not gamble.

You may need to consult a lawyer about certain liabilities involving your parent's care. Someone may be injured in your
home while assisting your parent. Nursing homes are extremely
nervous about their liability, and require release forms from next
of kin regarding bed rails and physical restraints. Whenever
injury or property damage is involved, a lawyer can help sort
out facts and regulations, and advise you accordingly.

A new area for litigation may emerge in the field of "patient
rights." Nursing homes are legally required to inform residents
of these rights upon their admission; we've referred to some of
these earlier in this book. The first several deal with the patient's
right to participate in the planning of his own treatment, to be
kept medically informed, and to be assured of confidentiality
concerning medical information. When the resident becomes
incompetent, the next of kin ought to become the parent's agent,
and should be kept similarly informed. This is not happening
as often as it should, and the denial of these rights may have to
be tested in the courts.

Insurance

If your parent carries no life insurance, you may want to
investigate the possibility of purchasing a small policy, perhaps
one that would cover funeral expenses.

Even term policies are expensive (and sometimes not available
after age seventy-five); you must judge whether they offer sufficient value for the premium. Blue Cross/Blue Shield sometimes
offers life insurance policies to senior citizens, as does the insurance affiliate of AARP.

Income Tax—For Your Parents

You may be required to file an income tax return for your
parent. IRS regulations change with each Congress, but pres-

ently (as of 1980, filing for 1979) a return must be filed if a single parent over sixty-five earned at least $4,300 for the taxable year, or at least $7,400 if both parents are living and are over sixty-five. Social Security, railroad retirement, and welfare benefits do *not* count toward this total; such income is *not* taxed (neither are life insurance proceeds). Thus, total income for tax reporting purposes must come from actual earnings, royalties, tips, or interest. Extra deductions may be claimed for being over sixty-five and for blindness.

When a parent dies, an income tax return must be filed on or before the usual April 15 deadline during the year following death. You file only if your parent would have been required to file on the basis of income, as described above.

I have not had to file income tax returns for either Paul or Anna.

For detailed information, ask your IRS office for a copy of publication 559—*Tax Information for Survivors, Executors, and Administrators*. This booklet not only gives helpful information on filing that final Form 1040, but it also gives guidance regarding estate taxes, if any.

Income Tax—For Yourself

If a parent (or some other dependent) lives with you and if you provide more than half of that person's support, you may claim that person as a deductible exemption.

To determine "dependent status," you are allowed to include prorated costs of housing and food for which you are not reimbursed.

If one or more members of the family share such costs, by agreement one person who provides at least 10 percent of the dependent's support may claim the exemption. However, only one person may do this. Each of the other members must file a written statement agreeing not to claim the exemption for that year. Form 2120 (*Multiple Support Declaration*) may be used for this purpose. The exemption may be claimed by other members of the family in subsequent years, if the criteria are met.

Remember to include medical expenses you incurred for your

parent, as well as transportation costs of taking your parent to see doctors and dentists, to clinics, or to therapy centers.

Social Security

One must apply for Social Security benefits; those monthly checks just don't begin to arrive automatically.

Your parent should apply at the nearest Social Security office, either in person or by telephone. Of course, you can assist in this process as needed. Find the address and telephone number in your telephone book under "United States Government."

Reduced benefits are available as early as age sixty-two. Full benefits begin when one reaches sixty-five. You should apply three months before the date you wish the benefits to begin.

Application for Medicare is made through your local Social Security office as well. This is also where you apply for "representative payee" status, if required.

Food Stamps

This program is helpful to qualified elderly persons who live independently or in certain home-care situations. Food stamps extend and expand a limited food budget.

Food stamps are a program of the U. S. Department of Agriculture, but are usually administered in individual states by welfare or human resources departments. Consult any of these offices for current information.

Discounts

Discounts also help senior citizens to stretch budgets.

Banks often make no monthly charge for checking accounts.

Bus lines (city and interstate) offer reduced fares.

Department stores and drug stores sometimes advertise a 10 or 15 percent discount to persons sixty-five or older. This can be a particularly large saving when prescription drugs are needed.

Some cafeterias offer a "senior citizen plate-of-the-day." A few restaurants are also beginning to promote discounts on noon or evening meals, sometimes adding a free meal or cake or champagne on the person's birthday.

Many state museums, art galleries, theaters, and concert series also offer discounts to those over sixty-five.

Personal Identification

Often a parent needs some kind of official identification for purposes of cashing checks or establishing new accounts. The most widely accepted identification seems to be driver's licenses, but older people who no longer drive do not have these. County offices and many city police departments now provide an official ID card, with photograph, for older persons who no longer drive. Usually these are free.

Voter Registration

Your parent may still want to participate actively in the democratic process. Keeping up with political campaigns—both national and local—is another way to keep up with reality.

Check with your county registration office about deadlines for registration.

If your parent is unable to write, you (the son or daughter) are allowed to register and sign for your parent. Your parent may then vote in person or by absentee ballot, which you request from your city clerk.

Con Games and Other Forms of Exploitation

The elderly are still considered fair game by unscrupulous entrepreneurs. It's a pity that another good English word—*confidence*—has been abused and now also connotes the meaning of "swindle."

Your local Better Business Bureau has pamphlets and current information about the more common rackets that may be operating in your city or county.

If your parents live independently, you should alert them to such risks and dangers.

Under no circumstances should your parent ever withdraw

savings from a bank or savings-and-loan association at a stranger's request. For example, someone may appear to be investigating an alleged embezzlement. Because someone in higher authority may be "involved," the stranger convinces his prey that the financial institution must not be informed; moreover, the immediate withdrawal of savings, delivered to a third party, will help the investigator find the "culprit." You are told there is no risk, that neither principal nor interest will be lost. Sometimes someone has found "a lot of money," but it will take someone else's money to "show good faith" to an employer.

There are variations on this game, but the scam still claims its victims. If your parent is ever approached with such a scheme, he or she should get in touch with you or the police as soon as possible.

Your parent should be wary of any home improvement "specials" offered by door-to-door salespersons. Roofing and painting still seem to be common ruses. Inferior materials are used or the job is never completed, but usually the price has been paid in advance to people with no local address.

Repairs should be made by reputable local firms. Responsible businesses will be happy to provide references and performance bonds. Checking with the Better Business Bureau or the Chamber of Commerce on persons soliciting work is also helpful.

Most cities now require licenses for any door-to-door solicitation for business or charity. It doesn't hurt to ask for the appropriate ID.

There are new laws protecting "consumer rights," and your parents should be aware that if they sign a contract in their home for any merchandise, they have the legal right to cancel that contract within three days.

Sometimes unordered merchandise is received through the mail, followed by bills and cunning letters. Often these are tied in with appeals for charities. Lots of greeting cards or handicrafts by supposed "native Americans" or "war-displaced refugees" are distributed in this way. So are books and raffle tickets. Such mailings are pure speculation on the part of the mailer. If the item was not ordered, it doesn't have to be paid for nor returned.

Estate Planning

Several elements of estate planning have already been mentioned, but some review and expansion might be helpful.

If your parent is wealthy, estate planning has probably already begun or is in process. However, even where large cash reserves or property holdings and investment portfolios do not exist, consideration should be given to alternatives that affect inheritance taxes. There may also be ways we can help ourselves as we approach our own retirement years.

In 1790, a member of the U. S. Congress is reported to have said that "the time will come when the poor man will not be able to wash his shirt without paying a tax."

"Death taxes" do exist. The federal government calls them "estate taxes." Most states call them "inheritance taxes."

At the time this book was printed, no federal tax was required on estates valued at $175,625 or less; the total could be significantly higher if marital deductions are included. In addition, the law allows for several deductions that can significantly reduce the "value" of a larger estate. Funeral expenses, legal and management fees, and bequests to charitable organizations are examples of such deductions.

State inheritance tax laws vary and do not always follow federal guidelines. If property is owned in several states, taxes for each state may be required.

However, both federal and state laws insist that appropriate reports be filed whether or not any tax is due. Such reports must usually be filed within a year after death, although some states direct that such reporting be made within nine months. Tax courts can be petitioned for an extension if "hardship" can be shown.

A sixty-thousand dollar limitation was imposed at the time the Tax Reform Law was passed in 1976. Increases have since been phased into the provision. The new level, cited above, may appear to be so large that it does not affect most of us. Because of inflation, this is no longer true. The value of residences or farms can easily be computed in the six-figure range. Many more of us, whether we like it or not, will have to concern ourselves with estate matters.

Since estate laws are complicated, to secure accurate and current information it is probably wisest to consult an attorney who specializes in estate planning and inheritance tax laws.

These are a few areas for you to consider.

Estate and inheritance taxes can be minimized; the law provides for this. These aren't tax "loopholes"; they are provisions the government expects its citizens to claim. This is difficult for us to do if we are neither legal nor tax experts.

Distinction is made between "separate" and "community" property. When a spouse dies, all "separate" property is subject to tax, while only half of "community" property is considered to be part of the estate.

There are laws that allow for marital deductions, or special large gifts made during the lifetime of both spouses. These are intended to add to the personal or "separate" estate of the other spouse, while at the same time providing certain gift tax advantages.

The estate can be reduced during one's lifetime by making certain gifts to friends or relatives. Gifts are not taxable up to a total of three thousand dollars per year. Gifts above that amount are taxable and must be reported on a *gift tax return*. Gifts made "in contemplation of death" (the legal term used to mean gifts made within three years prior to death) are subject to estate taxes, which are usually higher.

A grandparent might choose to distribute three thousand dollars or less to grandchildren each year. A larger amount could be given tax-free if *trusts* were established for the grandchildren (or great-grandchildren).

A parent might choose to make a gift of property to a family member or to a charitable organization. The gift would be taxed if given to an individual, but the tax would be based upon the market value of the property at the time of the gift. In an era of continuing inflation, it can be safely predicted that gift taxes on property will be less if paid *now* rather than paid *later* as estate taxes.

Your parents might want to consider making larger contributions to missions organizations or churches or other charitable groups. Such gifts must be reported if they exceed three thousand dollars annually, but they are not taxable and can be claimed as contribution deductions for federal income tax purposes.

Mention was made earlier of trusts. These can be "revocable" or "irrevocable," and they can help others while providing tax relief for the donor. Trusts should be established with the help of a professional.

Beneficiaries should be named in insurance policies as well as in mutual funds, where allowable. Depending upon the amount, insurance proceeds received by an individual may not be taxable. However, if they or similar proceeds are merely assigned to the "estate," estate and inheritance taxes will apply.

Most parents, no matter what their economic status, probably want to be able to leave something to someone else at the time of their death. You need to talk frankly about such hopes and wishes while your parents are still living.

Regardless of the amount of resources, your parent can do more good with funds and property now than later. This is simply a fact of tax life in our economic system. Make sure your loved one realizes this fact.

Another point to consider is liquidity or availability of funds. If it is known that estate and inheritance taxes will have to be paid, those taxes must be paid by a certain date and from re-sources in hand. Some funds should be readily available to the executor or administrator at least within a six-month period after death if property or securities are not to be prematurely sold, perhaps at a loss, merely to satisfy a tax lien.

Finances are a sensitive area of family life, as we said at the beginning of this chapter. You may have to overcome your own misgivings and reluctance about discussing decisions concerning money and property. You will simply have to marshall your facts, secure the professional advice you need, and risk the possible or imagined indictment of being self-serving.

By facing these realities soon enough, you'll really be doing a service for your parent and for those people and causes about which your parent has continuing concern.

Resources—Chapter 14

● *Legal Aid Societies* provide special services for the elderly.

● A *do-it-yourself kit* for planning your will is available from Hanley's, 22502 Orchard Lake Rd., Farmington, MI 48024.

● Get to know the people at your *Social Security office.* This is where your parent must apply for Social Security benefits and a Medicare card, where you apply for "representative payee" status, and where you report the death of Social Security recipients and apply for burial benefits. Look under "U. S. Government" in the white pages of your phone book.

● You should also become familiar with social workers handling *Aged, Blind, and Disabled* (ABD) programs. You'll learn about eligibility requirements for Medicaid, home-chore care, and nursing-home care. You may also learn about day activity centers and other experimental programs. ABD programs will likely be found under "State Government—Welfare" or "Human Resources" in the telephone book.

● If your parent is a veteran, review insurance, disability, and pension benefits with your *Veterans Administration* office. VA hospitals and convalescent homes are available to veterans with service-connected disabilities and illnesses. Other veterans may obtain medical services on a space-available basis. Death benefits are available to all veterans, and burial is possible in national cemeteries.

● The *American Association of Retired Persons* (AARP) is more than an advocacy group. It offers several reasonable supplementary health insurance plans and sells auto insurance as well. Prescription drugs at discount prices are offered. *Modern Maturity* is its elegant and informative publication. You can join as early as age fifty-five! AARP's address is listed at the end of this book.

Milam, Edward E., and D. Larry Crumbley. *Estate Planning After the 1976 Tax Reform Act.* American Management Association, 1978. Technical and comprehensive, but readable.

Kling, Samuel. *The Complete Guide to Everyday Law.* Chicago: Follett Publishing Co., 1970.

Poor, Henry V., ed. *You and the Law* (rev. ed.). Pleasantville, N.Y.: Reader's Digest Association, 1977.

15

Until Death Do You Part: Funeral Arrangements

Let us labor for the Master
From the dawn till setting sun,
Let us talk of all His wondrous love and care;
Then when all of life is over,
And our work on earth is done,
And the roll is called up yonder,
I'll be there.

—J. M. Black (1859-1936)

There is much more open discussion these days about death and dying, and that is truly a hopeful sign. Christians, especially, should never be reluctant about discussing death, not if faith is real and trusting. There can be no resurrection of the body without the death of the body.

Talk About Death

As our parents grow older, it's not only appropriate but essential that we talk through the implications of death and their preferences regarding a funeral service and burial. Talking through one's attitudes about death and the future life can be helpful to your parent and to you. There is considerable evidence that older people do want to talk about such subjects.

Although there are specific details to discuss, I feel they can be deferred until you have satisfied the need to talk about the fact of death itself. There may be apprehensions or affirmations, so try to deal with these first.

Talk About Wishes

When it's time to discuss specifics, you'll want to talk with your parent about his or her will. This doesn't have to be a morbid or self-serving exercise. If he or she hasn't made a will and is mentally capable of doing so, encourage your parent to prepare one with the help of a lawyer.

If your parent has made a will, find out the name of the lawyer who drew it, the location of the original, and who was named executor. The original copy of a will should not be kept in a safe-deposit box because these are usually sealed for several days or weeks by the court, following death. A *copy* of the will might be kept in a safe-deposit box, but the original should be in the hands of a lawyer, the executor, or a family member.

Discuss your parent's wishes for the disposition of special possessions and personal effects. A stamp collection, photographic equipment, an heirloom, a piano, or a favorite chair are the kinds of things that aren't specifically mentioned in a will, but about which there could be some understanding and agreement. Your parent's wishes could be set down in the form of a letter, signed by your parent, and kept with the original copy of the will. Such a letter could also contain specific instructions for the funeral.

After his death, it was learned that Franklin D. Roosevelt had left detailed guidelines for a simple and inexpensive funeral. That letter was found in a safe-deposit box, long after an elaborate and expensive state funeral had been held.

Talk About the Funeral

Take time to plan a funeral or memorial service. It may take more than one session to do this, although the discussion doesn't have to be drawn out. Just do it together.

You might read through one of the standard services found in the *Minister's Star Book* or in the manual of your church (*Book of Church Order, Book of Worship, Disciplines, Book of Common Prayer,* etc. Borrow a copy from your pastor if you don't have one).

While it is true that funeral services are for the living, we rarely take time to read the Scriptures and prayers of a funeral service with our own deaths in mind. Such a review can be a powerful moment for renewed and strengthened faith, for finding new courage, and for affirming our hope.

Your parent may be dissatisfied with a standard service; he or she may want something different or something more. In that case, write your own service together. Should there be celebration by way of music? If so, what music? What is your parent's favorite hymn? If a choir is available, what should they sing? What favorite Scriptures should be included? Should there be an affirmation of faith, such as a congregational reciting of the Apostles' Creed? What does your parent want said about himself or herself? What would your parent want to say to friends and loved ones who will be present? The process of developing a funeral service together can be a marvelous devotional experience as well as a practical decision for the future.

I recently shared in a funeral service that left me inspired and happy. Dr. DeWitt C. Reddick, under whom I had studied at the University of Texas and with whom I had occasion to work on various subsequent projects, died after a long illness. The printed order of worship included these elements: the Call to Worship, the Prayer of Confession (which all of us prayed), the Declaration of Pardon, the Ministry of the Word (during which there was a brief biography of Dr. Reddick), and the Prayers of the People. A soloist sang "How Great Thou Art." All of us sang—triumphantly, I thought—Martin Luther's "A Mighty Fortress Is Our God" and Bishop How's "For All The Saints."

The order of worship had this printed inscription:

WITNESS TO THE RESURRECTION
OF
JESUS CHRIST
on the occasion of the death of
DeWitt C. Reddick
who lived for the
glory of God

This in itself was a tremendous testimony and affirmation of faith, not only to us who believed but also to the many non-Christians who were present for that service.

This "witness to the resurrection" (which is the way Presbyterians now refer to a funeral service) ended with the organist playing Handel's "Hallelujah Chorus" as everyone went their separate ways.

The "Where" and "How" of Burial

Where does your parent wish to be buried? Close by? Beside a spouse, perhaps long since deceased and buried in a distant cemetery? Has a burial plot already been purchased?

Does your parent wish to be buried? Has cremation been seriously considered? This has theological as well as economic implications. Cremation is a clean, orderly method of returning the body to the elements. Except for two states (Massachusetts and Michigan), a casket is not required if cremation is done immediately. Embalming is not required if cremation is done within twenty-four hours after death. As for theological implications, ground burial and cremation both result in "dust to dust, ashes to ashes"; it is the Lord who restores life and promises a new body, along with a new heaven and earth.

Great emphasis has been placed in this country on ground burial and embalming. Now that space is scarcer around our cities, people may be buried in tiers above ground in vaults, such as has been done in many European countries for centuries. Ground burial is expensive because of the cost of land (and hillside plots command premium prices). Ground burial in most cemeteries now requires the additional expense of a concrete liner for the solid surface essential to "perpetual care" and heavy mowing machines.

Embalming is as old as Egypt, but little of it is done in such progressive Western countries as Germany and England. It is necessary if there is to be any viewing of the body. It is also necessary if the body is to be transported some distance for burial. Morticians (in America we call them "funeral directors") plead for embalming, affirming that the "restorative" process allows family members to deal better with their grief, remembering a loved one as he once was rather than as he was in the last stages of a degenerative disease.

How do religious convictions affect our accepted cultural practices? These are issues you might wish to discuss with your parent.

Should the service be held in a funeral chapel or a Christian church? You will be charged for the former, of course. Should there be a graveside service, too—or should there only be a

graveside service? Should there be a memorial service instead
of a funeral? Memorial services are held when the body is not
present due to accident, cremation, disposition to a medical
school, or simply by the wish of the decedent.

If your parent has been active and well known or has lived
and worked in several different locations, you may want to discuss the possibility of one or more memorial services in other
cities.

The "Living Will"

Perhaps you would like to discuss the making of a "Living
Will." If a person is terminally ill, he or she may not wish to be
kept alive by so-called "heroic" measures. Living Wills are not
legally binding instruments in every state, but they do carry
moral and personal weight.

The following is the text of a Living Will. Copies of this revised
version may be secured from *Concern for Dying* (see Address List
at back of book), which gave permission for its reproduction
here.

TO MY FAMILY, MY PHYSICIAN, MY LAWYER,
AND ALL OTHERS WHOM IT MAY CONCERN

Death is as much a reality as birth, growth, maturity and old age—it is
the one certainty of life. If the time comes when I can no longer take
part in decisions for my own future, let this statement stand as an
expression of my wishes and directions, while I am still of sound mind.

If at such a time the situation should arise in which there is no reasonable
expectation of my recovery from extreme physical or mental disability,
I direct that I be allowed to die and not be kept alive by medications,
artificial means, or "heroic measures." I do, however, ask that medication
be mercifully administered to me to alleviate suffering, even though
this may shorten my remaining life.

This statement is made after careful consideration and is in accordance
with my strong convictions and beliefs. I want the wishes and directions
here expressed carried out to the extent permitted by law. Insofar as
they are not legally enforceable, I hope that those to whom this Will is
addressed will regard themselves as morally bound by these provisions.

(Here one may insert specific statements, if desired, such as who is appointed to make binding decisions concerning medical treatment, mention of specific measures of artificial life support that are especially abhorrent—such as nasogastric tube feedings or mechanical respiration devices—the preference to live out last days at home if this does not jeopardize recovery to a meaningful, sentient life or impose an undue burden upon one's family, and any reference to donating tissues and organs as transplants.)

The statement is then signed, dated, and witnessed by two persons. Indication is made to whom copies were given; your physician must be one of these persons. It is suggested that a person review and initial this document annually, indicating the date. In this way it will be evident that the statement represents his or her continuing intent.

Donations

Many people now consider willing their bodies to medical schools for research or donating specific organs, such as eyes or kidneys, to eye or kidney "banks." A uniform donor card is available that is considered to be a legally binding will. It should be carried by the donor at all times. Additional information can be secured by writing to the American Medical Association, the Living Bank, or the Concern for Dying Educational Council (see Address List at end of book).

You might want to discuss whether your parent has a special charity, ministry, or mission program to which contributions might be made in lieu of flowers.

The more you know about your parent's actual wishes and thinking, the better.

Our Parenting Decisions

Anna is now too confused and unaware to discuss these matters intelligently; in her case we waited too long.

But Carolyn and I have had several conversations with Paul. He made it clear that if he died in Ecuador, he wanted to be buried there. That was a good decision. Anyone traveling overseas should carry some statement about such wishes. In case of death or accident overseas, the normal procedure is for the U.S. consul to return the body to the United States.

Paul also made it clear that if he died in the United States, he wanted to be buried next to his wife Berenice in Mt. Gilead, Ohio, where a family plot was already purchased. Because of this wish, we know he wants ground burial and he will be embalmed.

We know the hymns Paul wants sung at his memorial and graveside service. He wants costs kept to a minimum. He prefers that friends contribute to missions or the cause of distributing Scriptures instead of purchasing flowers.

Carolyn and I have made arrangements on the basis of this knowledge.

We have prepaid contracts with an Austin mortician for both Paul and Anna. We have chosen the type of casket. Morticians have been contacted in Ohio and in Illinois, and are included in the agreement.

A memorial service will be held for Paul in Cleveland in the church he once pastored and which has supported him over the years. Graveside services will be held for both Paul and Anna. Anna will be buried in Illinois, next to her husband, Anton, where we own a burial plot. Anna's service will be bilingual, using both English and Lithuanian, since some of her friends may be present whose knowledge of English is still minimal.

Because we have a burial contract we know the exact costs. And since the money is held in trust, the interest it earns should care for whatever increases are caused by inflation.

A burial insurance policy could accomplish the same objective.

Regular insurance proceeds will also pay such costs, of course. However, payment is often delayed. It would be wise to discuss financial obligations and schedule of payment with your mortician.

Having buried my father in 1949, spending far more on that funeral than we could afford or he would have wished, I believe Carolyn and I have made the right decisions regarding Paul and Anna. We have decided intelligently and calmly. We have not been pressured. We have benefited from the specialized service a mortician offers, and we found the one we dealt with sympathetic to our wishes and objectives. It will be much easier for us to proceed when this need arises in our lives. Furthermore, if anything should happen to Carolyn or me, if our parents should outlive us, plans for our parents' funerals are on file at each nursing home and can easily be carried out by someone else.

Other Details

Most states now have chapters of "Memorial Societies"—voluntary groups of people who seek to obtain dignity, simplicity, and economy in funeral arrangements through advance planning. You might find help from one of these.

Check on special death benefits that may be available to your parent. Social Security presently pays about $255 toward funeral expenses. The Veterans Administration provides up to $400 for veterans, and burial in a national cemetery can be arranged if certain requirements are met. A government headstone is also available. Medicare pays for final medical bills. Unions, pension funds, insurance, fraternal orders, and professional groups may also have special benefits to offer. If the cause of death was related to employment, workmen's compensation may allow certain death benefits

When a parent dies, you will probably want to notify immediate family, close friends, and former employer or business colleagues by telephone. Having a list in advance helps. More distant friends can be informed by letter. Notify insurance companies. If your parent owned a car and had automobile insurance, cancel it.

Arrange for family members or close friends to take turns answering the door or telephone, and keep a record of calls.

Write an obituary that could be sent to your parent's college alumni publication and/or other journals and newspapers where friends will learn about the death.

Check on debts. Some may be covered by insurance. It is helpful to have adequate and accurate financial records about your parent's business affairs.

Finally, a word about grave markers.

My father designed his own monument, which he intended to be a continuing reminder of his mission in life. He wanted an open Bible to show the words of John 3:16. Anna and I kept faith with his wish, and the monument stands in the Lithuanian National Cemetery in Justice, Illinois, just outside of Chicago.

Markers can be expensive, and sometimes unscrupulous sales tactics are used to pressure family members into buying something elaborate and expensive. Cemeteries—especially those providing so-called "perpetual care"—have grave marker requirements that limit material, size, and style.

Perhaps your parent has something special to say in this visible, public way.

Benjamin Franklin did. This is his self-written epitaph.

The Body
of
Benjamin Franklin, Printer
(Like the cover of an old book,
its contents torn out,
And stripped of its lettering and gilding)
Lies here food for worms.
Yet the work itself shall not be lost,
For it will (as he believes) appear once
more
In a new
And beautiful Edition
Corrected and Amended
by
The Author.

Resources—Chapter 15

● A "Consumer Survival Kit" (mentioned previously) called *The Last Rights: Funerals* is an excellent overview and discussion resource. Write Maryland Center for Public Broadcasting, Owings Mills, MD 21117.

● A bibliography of audiovisuals dealing with the topic "Living With Death" is found in the March-April, 1975, issue of *Medium*, published by the Institute for Jewish Life, Media Project, 65 William St., Wellesley, MA 02181.

● There is growing interest in memorial services as opposed to funeral services. Write the Continental Association of Funeral and Memorial Societies, 1828 L St., NW, Washington, DC 20036, for information about groups in your state.

● Many current seminars and books deal with the subject of death and dying. A book to begin with is *To Live Until We Say Goodbye*, by Elisabeth Kübler-Ross (New York: Prentice-Hall, 1978.)

● The *Living Bank* provides information about donating eyes, kidneys, and other organs. *New Eyes for the Needy* accepts metal and plastic frames, brown artificial eyes, and cataract lenses. *Concern for Dying* provides information about the Living Will and donation of organs for transplants. (See Address List at back of book.)

16

Visiting and Communicating With Elderly People

"The time has come," the Walrus said,
"To talk of many things:
Of shoes—and ships—and sealing-wax—
Of cabbages—and kings—
And why the sea is boiling hot—
And whether pigs have wings."

—Lewis Carroll (1832-1898)
Through The Looking-Glass

These days, when I visit, Anna rarely recognizes me as her son. As I have aged, I look more like my father, and I think Anna often thinks I am Anton, her husband of many years ago. Perhaps this should be expected despite her disability; she has known me as an adult for more years than she knew Anton as her husband.

Anna accepts Carolyn and appears grateful for her attention, but she doesn't know Carolyn is her daughter-in-law.

Paul does recognize us for who we are. He knows his other daughter, Esther, and her husband, Wally. He identifies his grandchildren and great-grandchildren from the pictures on his wall. Most of the time he can place the name of someone who writes to him. He receives information, but can't always respond. Aphasia shackles his tongue. His speaking vocabulary is limited, and sometimes they are not the words he needs to express his thoughts.

Anna and Paul live with severe communications handicaps; in this chapter I will describe some of the specific ways we have discovered to share life better with our parents.

It is often equally difficult to communicate with disabled people who are neither senile nor disoriented nor affected by a speech disorder. Experts in gerontology say depression is the primary emotional ailment of our aging relatives and friends. It, like pain or disability, can hinder the process of communication.

But when they are lonely, bewildered with surroundings, enduring discomfort, suffering pain, and perhaps trying to cope with a frustrating handicap, these are the times visits can be most helpful and meaningful.

Here are a few suggestions for relating to older friends and loved ones, particularly those who live in nursing homes or other institutions.

Reality Orientation

Social workers recommend that older people be "kept in touch" by way of "reality orientation" or "reality therapy," a fancy name for a rather simple procedure.

Whenever you visit a parent who is becoming more confused about himself or herself and life, at some point in the visit turn the conversation to some reality. Establish what day and date it is. Ask the person his or her name; if possible, get your parent to write it. At any rate, let your parent know by mentioning his or her name that you know the name and the name is theirs. Discuss the season of the year and the weather outside. Underscore where the parent is living—in what city and in what state, as well as the name of the nursing home. You might want to chat about some headline of the day. Establish who is president of the United States. Call attention to upcoming anniversaries.

A calendar on the wall—the bigger the better, perhaps a large one where you tear off each day's date—and pictures of the family help establish time and relationships.

Repeat these kinds of questions during each visit. It isn't childish or irrelevant. This is the substance of reality, and for a person who is disoriented the repetition is necessary and helpful.

To be sure, not every resident of a nursing home suffers from brain damage or some handicap that restricts communication. For those who are blessed with clear or clearer minds, conversation is no problem. All you need to do is ask a question about the home town or a garden or grandchildren, and you can sit back and listen. Your visit and the opportunity to share is no less important.

Negotiation and Forgiveness

I strongly believe that elderly people should be treated as adults and not as children. However, this is easier to believe than to practice, particularly when senility brings on *childlike* (not necessarily *childish*) behavior.

It's also difficult to maintain this adult-to-adult relationship as we assume the role of parent for our parent.

There may be a need for *negotiation,* when it is clarified that you must assume certain responsibilities for the other. This is a new relationship for both of you, and it may be necessary to make clear that you are no longer a child (you are probably in your fifties) and that your parent is no longer a parent in the way he or she once experienced that role. Treating each other and visiting each other as adults will help establish a foundation for this new kind of family partnership.

It's essential to come to new understandings in this emerging relationship with our parents—in other words, to negotiate—because we as children carry so much emotional baggage with us.

We remember our parents as they used to be. Perhaps we still think of ourselves as we used to be. We remember past slights and misunderstandings and instances of our own erratic behavior. We remember things we said and situations that haunt us. We need to forgive our parents, and often we may feel that our parents still need to forgive us.

Perhaps we can discuss these things with our parents. On the other hand, the event that so sears our memory may long since have been erased from theirs. This is not their problem or tragedy; it is ours.

This is when we must negotiate with our Creator, who knows us and our relationships. If we are to establish healthy, supportive ties with our aging parents, we as believing adults must turn over our residual or actual guilt and anger to God. He does forgive and He does heal. Only in this way can we go forward; indeed, how can we express and share love with anyone until we experience God's love?

For many of us this has been the beginning of hearing and accepting the good news.

Persons of Worth and Dignity

While your parent is still alert and involved with life, keep in mind that you are the visitor to his or her residence. When parents are confused or handicapped, it's easy and often necessary to "take charge." I must do so now where Anna and her care are involved. But I must not be as quick to check Paul's closet and drawers to see if things are in order, without first explaining to him what I want to do and asking his permission to do so. This is also part of having adult relationships with older people. Their dignity is fragile, and we must not damage it.

Be Consistent and Regular

Maintain a definite schedule. This doesn't mean you always have to visit on Mondays at four; there will be times when you'll need to visit on Tuesdays at noon instead. Some elderly people are still quite conscious of time and the clock; Paul is one of these. Deviations in schedule can be explained. It is the conscious decision and commitment to visit two or three times a week—or once a week, if the distance is considerable—that is good discipline for the visitor and fulfilled expectation for the person being visited.

Regularity is important, whether you visit in person or by telephone, letter, or cassette tape. Content may be important; I'm rather sure that quantity and verbosity is not. And I now suspect that in this area of fading relationships Marshall McLuhan is correct: The medium (the visit) is the message.

Don't give up visiting merely because visiting is difficult. Without your visit your parent or loved one would become more withdrawn and more depressed. You don't visit to be appreciated; you visit to demonstrate by your presence that you still care, to be of whatever help and support you can be.

A Few Suggestions for Visits

1) *Take advantage of nostalgia.* Prepare a book of snapshots relating to your parent's life. Ask for explanations or descriptions, and write these under the pictures. This could become a kind

of "This-Is-Your-Life" album that you can review whenever you visit, and that your parent will find captivating and amusing when alone. This is good reality orientation as well. Perhaps staff members will enjoy seeing it and getting to know your parent better.

An old magazine—one that's thirty or forty years old—can sometimes serve the same purpose. Looking at old advertisements and pictures, seeing the old styles and old cars, can trigger happy memories. The recently reprinted *1908 Sears Catalog* makes a great gift!

2) *Get your parent to talk about those memories.* When did Mother meet Father, and how? Where was their first home? What was it like? Build on past interest in sports or hobbies or vocation. Get your parent to talk; one of the best things you can do as a visitor is to listen. Patients are constantly being told what to do and where to go, and they don't have much opportunity to chat.

Bring a map with you once in a while—perhaps one of the United States or the world. Let your parent point out those states where he or she lived, or the countries visited.

3) *Share some exercise.* A walk down the corridor (outdoors is better if the weather cooperates) is always helpful. Choose one of the exercises from Chapter 12. If your parent is handicapped, massage unused muscles.

4) *Work on a gift.* There may be a small craft item you could work on together for a grandchild's or great-grandchild's birthday. You can choose from easy-to-make, economical leathercraft items, simple embroidery items, or paint-by-number posters. Working together can be fun, and the project might occupy part of several visits. Other activities are discussed in Chapter 13.

If there isn't interest in making something, or you are between projects, bring a simple puzzle along.

5) *Bring something to read.* If your parent is aphasic or withdrawn, remember that if you can't chat, you can at least read. Bring something that will hold interest and that can be read in small segments. Continue that reading with each visit. While cassette tapes of many fine books are available through libraries, your personal reading will bring special pleasure. If it's an old favorite, so much the better. Repetition is desirable. Reading can provide structure and substance to your visits. (Pastors might

keep this simple hint in mind. When words fail them—and they do—pastors can read, too.)

6) *Memorize a joke or two, and share these.* Visits among church-related people like Paul and Anna sometimes tend to be overly somber and even pompous. There is a line in the "Old Hundredth" psalm-setting about "Him serve *with mirth*, His praise forth tell!" Why not? There is precious little laughter in the lives of the sick and the handicapped. Bring back some joy into their lives. Carolyn and I have found the *Reader's Digest* invaluable for short articles, anecdotes, and humorous stories. With all due respect to scouting, *Boy's Life* jokes are corny enough and simple enough to almost always guarantee a chuckle.

7) *When you speak, you don't necessarily have to shout.* Sometimes it seems that we think every older person is deaf.

8) *Be prepared to be silent.* Planning things to do or say is desirable, but your visit won't be a disaster if nothing is said or done. Your parent may be drowsy or may not be feeling well. Or both of you may suddenly be caught up with past memories.

This is where tactile communication—speaking by way of touch—may be needed. I say very little to Anna as I push her wheelchair up and down the corridor or outside her building. There is little we can say to each other now, but I massage her back, I hold her hand, I brush her hair. The silent times are many.

Paul often seems content to be left alone. This was true when he lived with us, and I think it's still true in his new residence. He needs time to be alone, to meditate, to pray, or just to doze. It is his privilege.

Your parent may be morose, despondent, and withdrawn. At times you may even sense resentment. Accept these silent moods. All these things will pass.

Be content with the "now." Some older people may remember more of the distant past than the immediate past; they may remember little, if anything, of what transpired yesterday. But they do experience the immediate moment. They may perceive it differently than you do, but it is being experienced. The present is the common denominator, so enjoy it; this may be all that will be granted to you.

9) *Be bright.* Many things may be going wrong in the world, in

your family, or perhaps even in your perception of the quality of care being given to your parent. I don't believe that a visit to a parent is the appropriate time or place to ventilate such concerns. If your parent raises questions about family or care, then of course they should be faced and answered. But don't overload your kin with a lot of unnecessary worries or concerns. I certainly would avoid criticizing institutional staff or administration in front of parents. Such problems should be dealt with at the level where solutions are achievable, not where anxieties will be increased.

Be satisfied with the act of visiting. No great emotional, intellectual, physical, or spiritual breakthrough may occur. If it does, thank God for the serendipity—and return another time expecting again only the opportunity of being together for this particular and immediate moment.

10) *Those of us who are Christians find special strength in reading Scripture and in prayer.* Familiar biblical passages can be repeated. Prayer can be shared. I wish we would always feel free to pray. Not only is this valid "reality orientation," but it is precisely at such times that one can sense God's Spirit close by.

11) *Make your visit brief.* Sometimes it will be obvious that you shouldn't stay longer than ten minutes. So be it. At other times, things will go well for half an hour. Don't overdo and don't overextend. Leave something unsaid for the next visit; leave something to be completed the next time you're together. In my view, short, frequent visits are much better than long, occasional ones.

12) *Get to know some of your parent's friends in the nursing home and visit them.* Get to know the relatives of those friends, and visit them. Perhaps, in time, you could trade off visits; this will add visitors to both sets of parents. This could prove extremely helpful when you are away on vacation or are caught in an emergency and you need someone to look in on your parent.

There are many lonely souls in nursing homes who have no one to visit them. We can't carry the entire burden, but there may be one or two people besides our parent or parents who need us as a friend.

Giving Gifts

Gifts do not have to be limited to anniversaries and birthdays. In fact, as time goes on the significance of these occasions may be lost upon your parents. But the excitement of opening a gaily wrapped package never totally disappears.

We sometimes make a special event of giving a needed item of clothing—a new dressing gown or pair of pajamas, a colorful flannel shirt for colder days, perhaps a pair of slippers. Cologne or shaving lotion can be presented as a gift. Belts and wallets often need to be replaced.

Flowers are enjoyed. One rose from your garden can bring delight. A growing plant—preferably one that will blossom—makes a good gift. So might a flowerpot with potting soil and a hyacinth or tulip bulb or some seeds.

Some practical gifts might include a "blanket support"—a device to support a blanket over one's feet, giving a bit more room for movement—or a tray table that fits over the arms of a wheelchair. A hand massage unit or a small hydromassage unit for feet or bath would make a practical and therapeutic gift.

Mobiles that turn and reflect light, pictures, large photographs of family members, and posters can decorate a room and provide pleasant moments of diversion and thought.

Tabletop FM radios with easy-to-handle controls and cassette playback units make good gifts. Perhaps a small window fan would be helpful. If a television is not readily available, a personal TV set—preferably one in color and with a remote control device—would be a long-term, ongoing (and expensive) gift.

Visiting Is Your Responsibility

The burden of visiting your loved one in a nursing home is yours and will likely be carried out by you alone. If your parent lives with you at home, whatever socialization occurs will most likely depend upon what you design and engineer.

"Burden" may seem to be a harsh word, but I think it's reality. It doesn't have to mean hardship or vexing obligation. The burden can be light; it can become a challenge and an opportunity for growing compassion. But this responsibility also can become tedious and frustrating, and to me that means "burden."

I think it's healthy to recognize this fact.

Carolyn and I are the only persons from the "outside" who now visit Anna. Paul has made a few new friends at Trinity Home; some are residents and some are residents' relatives who have adopted him. However, he receives few visits from friends of previous associations.

Trust Your Instincts

Our threshold of pain and frustration is easily lowered as we review check lists, listen to suggestions, and even read books such as this one. We ought to consult the experts. We should try to listen to what friends are saying.

But we live with a daily reality that doesn't always conveniently fit the categories we read about. It's easy to become bewildered and to feel guilty. Since the responsibility of caring for our parents is ours, there may come a time when we have to square our shoulders and do it our way, risking setbacks and perhaps even failure, but finding some strength and confidence in the knowledge we have gained about our own loved ones. This is when we have to trust our own instincts.

Example: Some experts claim that one-to-one visits are best, that when there is more than one visitor a group is formed and the closeness of two people conversing and sharing is lost. Perhaps. But Carolyn and I have often visited our parents (and other friends in hospitals and nursing homes) together, and we have not sensed that a diverse climate was created. The important thing was the visit.

Another example: Well-meaning friends can throw you a curve. They don't often visit your parents, but when they do they'll telephone to report. Of course this is thoughtful and welcomed. I think these friends want us to feel good; they want to give a positive report. But sometimes it's difficult to recognize whom they are describing!

I've indicated that Paul is aphasic. Occasionally I've received a call that began, "Paul is really improving; I understood almost everything he said."

The first time this was reported, it troubled me greatly. Was this person talking about the same Paul I knew? He had lived in our home for nearly two years, and we had had daily contact. Now I was visiting him several times a week. I knew *I* couldn't understand everything Paul was trying to say. Was I insensitive, or too close to the situation?

You see, conversing with Paul is often like playing a game of "twenty questions." One tries to determine subject (is it animal or vegetable?), the geography of the subject, and the time frame. I have probed and pondered for half an hour over something I thought was deeply theological or financial, only to discover finally that Paul was merely concerned about having some extra dollar bills in his wallet or knowing where his handkerchiefs had gone. This kind of conversation can wear you out, but afterwards you can laugh about it together.

I think Paul's well-meaning friends are so relieved to hear an occasional word from Paul that they understand that they grasp this as something symbolic, perhaps making more of it than they should. Or they may be so disturbed by their own inability to communicate and to understand that they leave after the first recognizable word, wanting to feel as good as possible about a frustrating experience.

A third example: Once you have decided upon long-term care for your parent (usually after consultation and urging from your physician), a friend with raised eyebrow will ask in a tone that sounds accusing, "Well, how *is* your Dad?" Most likely, we've misinterpreted his gesture and tone. But we must learn to live with the risk of some people not fully understanding our decision and misinterpreting our motives.

A final example: It's easy to be overwhelmed by the professional hierarchy in long-term health-care institutions. You can so easily be "put down" as a mere layman. If you observe conditions and practices that you question and that affect the care of your loved one, be assertive. Some things in life are too important to entrust totally to the hands of professionals. Trust your instincts.

Over the months and years, Carolyn and I have acquired a sixth sense in communicating with Paul and Anna. Both are different people with different problems, but somehow we do reach them from time to time, and they reach out to us. Perhaps this sixth sense is really instinctive among people sharing love.

Communicating With Aphasics

Aphasia is defined as a total or partial loss of the power to use or understand words. It is often the result of a stroke or other brain damage, and presents special problems for both visitor and victim.

Expressive aphasics are able to understand what you say; *receptive* aphasics are not. Some victims may have a bit of both kinds of impediment.

Paul is an *expressive aphasic.* We are able to read to him, he watches television, and he tries to participate in singing and in the repetition of familiar Scripture passages. His difficulty is communicating to us those feelings and words that are important to him. Our difficulty is trying too soon to anticipate what he wants to say, completing sentences for him without allowing him enough time to struggle with his own words.

Perhaps you remember how it felt when a word or name eluded you; you explained your embarrassment by saying that the word was "on the tip of your tongue." It probably was. This is the condition expressive aphasics experience most of the time; most of the words they want to speak are on the tips of their tongues, but they cannot be called forth.*

Speech therapists attack the problem by working with phonics and those sounds the patient has greatest difficulty with. Large picture cards are used to help rebuild vocabulary; often the therapist identifies synonyms that the aphasic patient can speak more easily. It is a slow and precise process. Some speech therapists do not welcome extra "drill work" by nonprofessionals; others encourage this, but want to direct and monitor your work.

Picturegram grids are sometimes prepared for aphasics. These are used as "fill-in" answers to the requests of "I need" or "I want"; the patient merely points to the appropriate drawing. This tool has not worked out for Paul.

To help Paul communicate with visitors and fellow residents,

---

*A most helpful book for me in understanding the brain damage of Anna and Paul was *Stroke* (New York: W. W. Norton, 1977) by Charles Clay Dahlberg and Joseph Jaffee, both physicians (one of whom is a psychiatrist who suffered a stroke with resulting paralysis and aphasia).

I wrote up a kind of ID card for him. We discussed the draft, and I typed the text on a three-by-five index card. (In fact, I typed up two copies—one for his pocket and another to keep as a spare.) This is the text we agreed upon.

My name is Paul Young. I was born near Pittsburgh in 1893. I accepted Christ as my Savior in my teens and felt called to serve Him. In 1918 I went to Ecuador as an evangelist and pastor. I am ordained as a Baptist minister and served the Christian and Missionary Alliance. Later I directed the United Bible Societies' work in Ecuador.

In July, 1976, I suffered a stroke that has left me with two handicaps: a paralyzed right side and "aphasia" (a speech problem). I do understand you when you speak. You will have difficulty understanding me, but as we talk together you may understand a few of my words and thoughts.

I have two daughters (and seven grandchildren and five great-grandchildren). Esther Howard lives in Columbia, Maryland. Carolyn Gillies lives nearby in Austin.

I do appreciate your visit. Talking to people has always been a big part of my life. Tell me about yourself. Tell me some news. Tell me a good joke. If you have time, I would be grateful if you would read something. Perhaps we could have a prayer together.

God bless you. And thank you.

The message, typed double-spaced, fills both sides of the card. Paul seems happy with this conversational tool. It allows him to tell others who he is and what is important to him. It keeps him from becoming a non-person, which is easy to become when you are bound to a wheelchair and are unable to communicate readily. It opens opportunities to look at books or scrapbooks or mementos.

Since Anna now speaks only gibberish, she too is a kind of aphasic.

For her, Carolyn and I prepared a small photo album with pictures of herself and Anton, our family, her grandchildren, various places she lived during her lifetime, and some of her friends. We also typed captions beside each photograph.

Anna is sometimes amused by the album, but probably doesn't relate to it much anymore. However, the album has been invaluable in the nursing home; many nurses and aides have looked at it and in this way have gained respect for Anna's life and accomplishments. I think it provides her with a measure of status and dignity she might not otherwise enjoy.

Visiting Through Correspondence

Writing is a real ministry of love and sharing. Many of the preceding suggestions relating to personal visits apply equally well to written correspondence.

It is necessary for Carolyn or me to read Paul's and Anna's mail, since they cannot. I am grateful for the small cadre of friends who continue to write even though they receive no response from either Paul or Anna except as Carolyn or I write to them.

We maintain a list of some one hundred names for both Paul and Anna. At least twice a year, either Carolyn or I mail some kind of communication to these friends. We want to inform them about Paul and Anna, but we also hope our writing will "prime the pump," resulting in some kind of written response.

Each has a dozen or so faithful friends who do take time to write letters and remember anniversaries.

Often only a card is sent, but this is signed by members of a prayer group or a Sunday School class or some organization with which Paul or Anna once had contact. Paul especially enjoys trying to place names with faces in his memory.

Some of the letters are outstanding. They are written in the style of personal conversation. In chatty fashion, the correspondents tell of their experiences or they recall some past shared event. Memories are awakened, and friendships are reaffirmed.

A few letters never should have been written and mailed. Fortunately, there are not many of these and I use considerable editorial judgment when I read them, *if* I read them. These are the letters that go into pages of detail about family who are unknown to any of us. Some convey gossip or minutiae of dissension in family or local church. Some catalog personal ailments. A few decry the abuses of government or ventilate their suspicion of conspiracies everywhere. Sad to say, I've even seen a letter or two in which the writer questioned God's dealing with Paul or Anna, wondering what evil was done or what demon may still be in control. These are modern-day "Job's friends."

Of course, letters do not have to contain only "sweetness and light." There is a place for relating significant news, some of which may well be tragic or disappointing. It may be that a situation is so serious that the writer desires to request prayer for its solution or resolution.

But potential letter-writers should try to avoid the doom-and-gloom habit, the petty, and the irrelevant. Goethe asked that we spare him our doubts; he had enough of his own already. St. Paul urged us to rejoice *always*.

The White House, with volunteer help, has been sending birthday greetings to persons eighty years or older (and to couples celebrating fiftieth wedding anniversaries). Send your request, with the name and address, thirty days before the birthday or anniversary date to Greetings Office, The White House, 1600 Pennsylvania Ave., Washington, D.C. 20500.

Record Your Correspondence

Instead of writing a letter, consider recording a cassette tape. Your voice makes it a kind of personal visit.

If you've never recorded a "living letter," make a trial recording and listen to it before mailing your first tape. The microphone is a sensitive instrument even on the cheapest recorders and it may reveal more of your feelings than you realize. If you're tired and depressed, you will *sound* tired and depressed. If you're happy and enthusiastic, your smile will be heard. Take time to use this medium effectively. You'll improve with practice; everyone does.

Cassette tapes should be conversational, lively, and brief. Imagine the person sitting in front of you as you speak. That's the secret of good announcers who sound so natural. Be brief; even professional narrators can put a person to sleep within half an hour.

I recommend that you discipline yourself by using the C-20 type of cassette, which provides ten minutes per side or a total of twenty minutes. You might even experiment with the idea of conversing and/or reading for five minutes or so, and then saying something like this: "Why don't we stop the tape here for today? Just leave everything the way it is, and we'll continue our visit tomorrow." Include some humor, anecdotes, and perhaps some continued story or book reading.

Even though Carolyn and I visit our parents regularly, we too are beginning to use cassette tapes. Both of us are recording books that Paul can add to his other listening. Because we are reading material we know interests him, we think we can extend our visits beyond the time we are physically present.

Resources—Chapter 16

● I've mentioned the journal called *Issues*, published by the United Church of Christ, which suspended publication in mid-1980. The Spring, 1979, issue was devoted to the topic of "Looks Can Kill: The Rights and Needs of Disabled People." Perhaps you could secure a copy from a UCC pastor or church library.

Dahlberg, Charles Clay, and Joseph Jaffe. *Stroke.* New York: W. W. Norton, 1977. (See note about this book on p. 178.)

17

The Religious Community's Ministry to the Aging

> *Renew Thy church, her ministries restore:*
> *Both to serve and adore.*
> *Make her again as salt throughout the land,*
> *And as light from a stand.*
> —Kenneth L. Cober (1902-   )

> *Dear Mother, dear Mother, the church is cold,*
> *But the ale-house is healthy and pleasant and warm.*
> —William Blake (1757-1827)

I must admit to a bias from the outset.

I am not impressed with institutional activity regarding older citizens—and I include secular organizations, colleges and universities, governmental agencies, and churches.

Curiosity exists. Some commitment is apparent. Some inquiry is being made. But very little is being done with and for older persons.

A major denomination that decides something ought to be done sets up a task force to study the problem, oblivious to what other denominations have already studied and reported.

A welfare department contracts with universities to do research or issues grants to groups that wish to experiment with new approaches, but the departments themselves rarely get involved with testing their own ideas, experimenting, and actually working with and being with the people to be served.

We are heavy on theory and light on ministry.

The church has defined and analyzed "mission," but has forgotten how to be *involved* with mission. In my view, the church has decided its priorities should be local and its ministries primarily directed to its youth and to a young, preferably affluent, middle-management constituency.

What's Being Done

Honest and able people are struggling to discover God's will for the church and its ministry to the elderly. These are some of the things being done.

Meals-On-Wheels. Churches provide volunteers and kitchens to prepare hot meals that are delivered to shut-ins or to activities centers. Government funds are available to support such services, if desired and requested.

Day-Care Centers. Some churches provide facilities and space to neighborhood groups or to governmental agencies for daytime activities for senior citizens. A hot, nutritious noon meal is provided, either delivered or cooked on the premises. If government funding is accepted, the meals are free. Those churches wishing to maintain traditional separation of church and state finance such programs on their own, or make a nominal charge for meals. Social workers tend to dislike the term "day care," but this often best describes the nature of the center. Such centers provide a pleasant, stimulating environment, often into late afternoon.

Special Events. A weekly or monthly luncheon and program is arranged in some churches just for its senior members and their friends. Sometimes an excursion is arranged, such as a visit to a museum, a nature center, or a zoo.

Paul has become acquainted with a fantastic rural church—Palm Valley Evangelical Lutheran Church, near Round Rock. Its members visit Trinity Home regularly, but they also reverse the process by bringing a group of residents from the home to the church once a month for a meal and fun and fellowship. Paul loves it. His own church roots are really rather shallow, and he now considers this beautiful old Swedish church *his* church. At least I think he does, because he likes us to drive past it and points to it with pride.

Visitation. A few churches record their Sunday morning or evening services and distribute these on cassette tape to shut-ins, some of these in nursing homes.

Church-owned facilities such as Trinity employ a resident chaplain who not only carries on a regular worship program, but also visits the "shut-ins" within the home, including frequent opportunity for them to share Communion in their rooms.

One retired Air Force chaplain has appointed himself a kind of honorary chaplain to three different nursing homes, which he visits regularly.

The Scott Memorial Baptist Church of San Diego employs an associate minister for its six hundred members who are past the age of sixty.

Some churches adopt a nearby nursing home. Pastors and lay members share the responsibility for leading a monthly (or weekly) worship service or Bible class. Youth groups present programs, and individual youths get to know individual residents, returning for personal visits whenever they can to perform small chores, read, or write letters for their new older friends.

Summer Camps. A group of churches contracted to use a church camp for oldsters. The charge of one hundred dollars per week included transportation from the New York City area and all meals. The traditional camp activities were available—games, sports, crafts, swimming—and there was plenty of opportunity for relaxing, making new friends, eating good food, and enjoying the outdoors.

Transportation. Many churches use buses to transport senior members or residents of retirement centers to worship services or special meetings. Sometimes transportation is provided through a corps of volunteers who use their larger cars for this purpose. Transportation is also provided to day activities centers.

Advocacy. A few denominations incorporate some focus upon older persons in the development of their church school curriculum or in "church and society" programs and policies. An excellent channel for this kind of focus is the Episcopal Society for Ministry on Aging. Some church state councils or conferences have held seminars on aging problems and ministries. The Southern Baptist Convention gives this issue its attention through its Christian Life Commission. United Methodists and Lutherans also make special commitments to the elderly.

The preceding has been a quick overview of what the church appears to be doing for its older members. It's not an insignificant list, but I truly wish it were longer.

Why More Isn't Done

I believe the church's ministry is truncated when it basically ignores a vast segment of its membership, and I think this is due to a serious malaise in the North American church.

Again my bias will show. I said earlier that most church leaders seem to minister primarily to the rising middle-level management person and family. *Stewardship* is the name of this process that determines policies and programs of denominations and local congregations.

Middle-level (and upward-rising) management is the main source of income and continuing growth, and the U.S. church is as committed to growth as is the U.S. corporation.

Children's and youth programs are fostered and encouraged insofar as these are demanded by the family. Social action programs are carried out only as these are approved and sanctioned by the local power structure of the church.

For the most part, the elderly are forgotten. Their pledges are small or nonexistent, so they generate little income for the church. They are rarely appointed to official boards and committees; consequently, their wisdom and experience (and sometimes expertise) is lost to the total community of believers. At best, the elderly are appeased; at worst, they are merely tolerated. There are exceptions, of course, but I am sufficiently cynical to suspect that the exceptions often relate to the hope of bequest or to the relationship of some older person to an active younger executive.

This is a heavy and a serious indictment. So be it. I happen to believe the church will be judged on its commitment to mission and service to *all* the members of Christ's body.

What More Could Be Done?

Here are several suggestions as to how many churches could be ministering to elderly people.

1) *Expand pastoral care.* Pastors have traditionally spent a good portion of their time visiting the sick and shut-ins, although much of this may now be ritualized in routine visits to hospitals. I wonder whether pastors make any more house calls these days than doctors do.

Following her hip operation, Anna was accidentally discovered by my former Presbyterian pastor. I suspect he found the family name in the card index the hospital provides. He stopped for a quick word and a prayer—and Anna, of course, did not know him and was already confused. Anna is a Baptist, but no one visited her from the Baptist church she had attended. Nor did my own pastor follow up—in the hospital, later in the nursing home, or even by way of inquiry to Carolyn or me.

Paul's experience with pastors has been a bit more felicitous, but only moderately so. The local Christian and Missionary Alliance pastor visited Paul about five times over the two-year period he lived in our home. A youth group came by to carol one Christmas. The pastor's successor has visited Paul once in the nursing home (once in fifteen months). To be fair, I should add that my own Presbyterian pastors have yet to visit him, either in our home or at Trinity.

And yet Paul has not been without pastoral visits. Occasionally, a missionary colleague has taken time off from a Texas tour to seek Paul out and chat and pray with him. Trinity Home's Lutheran chaplain not only sees Paul daily in chapel, but he stops by his room for frequent visits. Paul is really more fortunate than most of his age and condition.

I know that pastors are busy and can't do everything that is expected of them. And lay members should accept their own responsibility for visiting and sharing, for they too are to be "ministers" according to the Protestant understanding of the Bible.

Nevertheless, our elderly—and especially our elderly who are bedridden and handicapped—need care. They need to see and touch their local shepherd once in a while. They need to partake in the sacrament of Communion.

I'm glad that many pastors are better preparing themselves with special courses in counseling. Some are learning more about geriatrics. But I would like to challenge pastors—and elders—to do more "field work." "I was sick," said our Lord, "and you visited me. I was in prison and you came to me" (Matt. 25:36).

2) *Develop a strategy for ministering to older people in your congregation.* Sometimes we avoid or defer problems by setting up task forces, but here is an authentic opportunity to set up a study group that should include oldsters. Identify your older members, survey their interests, and determine ways to meet their special needs within and without the church building. Plan for people and money to help meet these needs.

3) *Develop a day-care program.* If your church presently operates or sponsors a day-care center or a kindergarten for children, consider the possibility of adding a day activities program for senior adults. The programs would probably remain separate, although there could be opportunities for wholesome and creative interaction between the generations.

4) *Organize a senior-citizens center.* Such a center doesn't have to be linked to a children's day program, of course. Neither does it have to be located in your church. Storefront locations in shopping malls might be the ideal site for such activity centers, right in the middle of the modern marketplace. Older people who live alone but are still able to get about need a place where they can socialize, where they feel they are still part of the mainstream of life, where they can find someone to talk to—perhaps someone who might be willing to help with a problem or offer some advice—and where they can share a cup of coffee or tea or soup. Senior-citizens centers don't have to be mere *recreational* facilities. Many oldsters are asking for more than recreation; they want challenge and stimulation as well.

Such centers might be sponsored by a local council of churches, a ministers' alliance, a cluster of like-minded churches, or a single congregation.

5) *Adopt a nursing home.* Identify the nursing homes within your immediate "parish" and determine which one needs help the most. Become involved with it and its residents. Talk to the administrator and the activities director. Discover ways volunteers from your church can be of ongoing help. Sponsor parties. Provide transportation. Arrange for excursions. Assist with shopping. Find those special few who never have visitors, who might thrive and even blossom with a bit of personal attention. Bring

those who are active and able to your church school or service. Make this a churchwide "adoption program." Involve officers, men's groups, women's groups, and youth.

You'll find opportunities for worshipping and witnessing together, but let these ministries grow out of a basic concern for people in the special location God has assigned to you.

6) *Involve more older members.* The elderly need to be needed, too. How and where can they be included in your congregation or in your church's outreach to the community? They ought to be represented on official boards and working commissions or committees. Some should be teaching Sunday school classes (and not necessarily just teaching peers). Others could manage and staff the nursery. Some could organize a food pantry for the transient needy, or a book-and-gift store (perhaps selling handicraft made by senior citizens or by Third World people).

7) *Provide telephone reassurance.* Many churches offer a daily recorded meditation or a "dial-a-prayer" ministry. Telephone answering devices are now readily available and inexpensive. A special recorded message might be prepared daily just for shut-ins or older people. Better still, maintain and staff a "hotline" that older people can call whenever they feel the need or the urge. Knowing someone will always be ready to listen and perhaps be able to help is a tremendous reassurance for fearful and bewildered people, helping them fight the demon of depression.

8) *Make your church more accessible* to older people, particularly those who are handicapped. Churches should be barrier-free. Build a ramp at one of your entrances so people may enter easily in their wheelchairs. Modify your seating arrangement somewhere in the sanctuary so people can transfer easily from wheelchair to pew or seat—or so they can simply remain seated in their wheelchairs without disturbing traffic or sight lines for others (perhaps a pew could be removed).

Provide hearing-aid devices. Remodel your rest rooms. One stall should have wider doors (so a wheelchair can enter) and sturdy grab bars. Raise one of the sinks so a person in a wheelchair can get close enough to wash his hands. Make it easier and safer for older people to get from one level to another. Ramps may be a possibility. Perhaps an elevator should be considered.

Look at your facilities through the eyes of a handicapped

person. Much can be done where you are with what you have, without costing a fortune. More can be done if you insist on barrier-free access when you design a new building.

The American Lutheran Church now denies low-interest loans to new churches whose building plans do not meet the needs of the physically handicapped. It's a policy other denominations could copy.

9) *Make occasional large gifts.* There are many creative ways of using money to provide special gifts to a nursing home or retirement center.

Sometimes only a good piano—or an extra piano—is needed.

A large-screen TV set might be needed, or your church or group might consider paying for cable TV installation and its monthly charges.

Institutions might need a good projection screen. Make it "lenticular" while you're at it; it's more expensive, but the images will be brighter.

A videocassette recorder would be a fine investment. Not everything on TV is froth, as I've said elsewhere. Many good programs—*National Geographic* specials, classic motion pictures, and documentaries—are aired in the late evening when many nursing home residents are already in bed or on their way to bed. The capacity for recording such programs for in-house "rebroadcast" at a more convenient time would be a great asset. (One of your members may already own a videocassette recorder and might volunteer to do such recording at home; in this case, some kind of playback unit would be required for the nursing home.)

You might want to invest in two videocassette recorders—one for the church and one for the nursing home. Add an inexpensive video camera and record the special programs presented at your church—youth programs, musical specials, visiting evangelists, Bible teachers, or missionaries. Record special Christmas programs and worship services. These could be played back at the nursing home whenever convenient.

Once you own a camera, you could take it to the nursing home and record some of the residents; get them to talk about themselves and their memories. They will love to see and hear themselves, and you might want to show these "programs" to people in your church or group. This would be a way to better understand the needs and status of older people who require special care.

Another large gift might be a van that could be used by various groups in the church, but that would also be available to transport older people from retirement centers, homes, or even nursing homes to special events at your church or elsewhere. If the van were equipped with an electric and/or hydraulic lift, people could be transported while sitting in their wheelchairs. It would cost a lot less than a new pipe organ!

10) *Provide housing.* Consider construction of a new facility or purchase of some existing facility for housing retirees or convalescing patients. Your group or church may qualify for federal funding.

If predictions about the twenty-first century are on target—if our senior population will indeed double within fifty or sixty years—then the church must begin *now* to plan for an expanded and *total* ministry.

Leading Worship in Nursing Homes

I hope you'll have the opportunity to lead a worship service in a nursing home sometime. It's a good experience.

I've probably attended a couple hundred such services—listening with Anna or Paul, leading the singing, playing the piano, and sometimes speaking. I have a few impressions of what "works" and what doesn't.

Services should be brief, no longer than half an hour. Nursing home residents become restless. Some have to visit the bathroom frequently. The attention span for most is limited.

Residents love to sing or to listen to other people sing. Use large-print hymnals if you can secure them. You can mimeograph your own hymn sheets, using the largest typeface typewriter you can find. Or use an overhead projector with a transparency of the words. You don't have to sing all the verses! It's hard not to do that when people ask for a familiar hymn like "Amazing Grace," but I think it's far better to sing one or two verses of several hymns and gospel songs than to sing all the verses of just one or two songs. Hymn sings, without preaching, are great for an afternoon or evening.

Include the residents whenever and however you can. Repeat the Lord's Prayer or Psalm 23 together. Ask for prayer requests. Use a "bidding prayer" format occasionally; invite people to pray with you for specific things, situations, and persons. Allow time for silences; not everyone wants to share and participate verbally.

Speak briefly. Perhaps there is something you could read or a story you could tell. I've used many devotionals written for family worship and for younger children, and these seem to have been well received.

I've sat through several painful worship services in nursing homes where the visiting pastor rambled on for thirty minutes or more. Sometimes it seemed he was reading all the verses under a given subject from the *Thompson's Chain Reference Bible.* I once suffered through forty minutes of exhortation on the joys of tithing—probably the most inappropriate topic for that particular audience that could have been chosen.

I've also sat through some well-meant efforts to mass evangelize nursing home residents. I'm sure there are people in nursing homes who need to make personal commitments to the Lord and who are able and competent to do so. But to me, the extended "invitation" seems inappropriate in the nursing home setting; it is tiring for restless, disoriented residents and it can become manipulative and even trite. Personal evangelism through counseling and visits would be much more effective, I think.

You might want to experiment with audiovisuals. Many filmstrips of Bible stories would stimulate interest and hold attention. If you don't have a filmstrip projector but have access to a slide projector, you can cut up older filmstrips frame by frame and insert each into half-frame slide mounts (available in most photographic supply stores). These can then be projected as slides. If you're a photographer, you probably have many slides in your files that would illustrate a psalm or a hymn.

Give the gift of divine comfort. There is biblical mandate to comfort God's people, and nursing home residents are in much need of this reassurance.

I think of Anna. She who once sang so beautifully no longer sings. She does not even attempt to repeat the Lord's Prayer. She is too restless now to sit through even a brief service. God still loves her, despite her failing mind. Somehow, she needs reassurance of that fact. And there are lots of Annas in nursing homes.

Don't rush off when the service is finished. Even if you are a layman, as I am, the residents think of you as the visiting "pastor." Your handshake, your conversation after the service, your tap on the shoulder, your embrace, and your smile are all ways—for some, the only ways—of communicating God's love in that particular setting and moment. If you're a frequent visitor, you'll be learning a few names. Use them; people are pleased when you call them by name.

Treating older people as special people of God is how the church's ministry to the aging will take substance and be authentically relevant.

Resources—Chapter 17

● Your denominational judicatory (conference, synod, diocese, etc.) office can provide you with information about special committees, task forces, and seminars related to ministries to the aging.

● One such agency is the *Episcopal Society for Ministry on Aging*,which provides consulting services to local parishes and conducts training seminars. (See Address List at the back of this book.)

● The *American Bible Society* prints Bibles and Scripture portions in large-print editions. *Lutheran Braille Workers* produces hymnals, Scripture portions, and tracts in large print. Addresses are in the back of this book.

● Augsburg Press, Hope Publishing, and Lillenas all sell hymnbooks (or collections) in large-print or "oversize" editions. For information, consult your religious bookstore.

● If you're looking for meditations to read to groups, look at the books by Robbie Trent and Phillip Keller. *You're Only Old Once,* by Catharine Brandt (Augsburg), is also helpful.

18

Parenting Requires Learning: A Personal Reflection

Remember also your Creator in the days of your youth, before the evil days come, and the years draw nigh, . . . before the silver cord is snapped, or the golden bowl is broken, or the pitcher is broken at the fountain, or the wheel broken at the cistern, and the dust returns to the earth as it was, and the spirit returns to God who gave it.

—Ecclesiastes 12:1–7

Isn't it true that we became better parents through the process of being parents? Our third child had more experienced parents than our first.

We also learn to be parents of our own parents. May I share a few highlights of what I have learned?

The Gift of Dignity

I have learned that one of the greatest gifts I can give my parents in their declining years is the gift of dignity. Despite the winding down of body and mind, each is a person with a history, with values, and with needs. I must provide them as much dignity as I can in their ongoing lives and as we prepare for their deaths.

Caretaking

I have learned that I am a caretaker, not a custodian. Providing care—or enabling someone else to provide care—is a large and gracious responsibility given to me by my Lord.

Availability

I have learned that I must be available.

I must regularly and personally visit my parents. No matter

how forgetful they become, they must see and touch me and I must see and touch them.

This availability affects my life-style, but I must accept this with grace and joy. I must now plan my trips and vacations with my parents in mind. It is no longer possible to place them "out of sight, out of mind." I've purchased a telephone answering device not only to keep in contact with my editors and clients, but also to keep in touch with both nursing homes, wherever I may be.

I must also be available to my immediate family. I must live my own life with the responsibilities and adventures I share with Carolyn and, to a lesser degree now, with my children. However, I now also have grandchildren who need contact with their grandfather.

Communicating

Communication has been my livelihood and profession for many years. I have instructed others in it. But I have had to rethink my understanding of communication as I have tried to communicate with my parents. I am still learning.

I have learned to listen, to interpret strange sounds, to go beyond the gibberish to understand what is being conveyed through gesture and mood. To listen in this way means to learn to relax, not to assume too much, and to be content when very little is understood.

I have heard myself speak jargon. We all speak it—that special language or vocabulary we use in our work and daily lives that others may not understand. Much of what we say makes little sense to people who do not share our environments nor our professional interests.

Thus, when I speak to Paul about my work or a book I am reading or a seminar I attended, I must be careful not only that he is actually interested in the subject matter, but that he can understand the language I use to describe it.

Sometimes, just in time, I have become aware that I am merely flaunting my new insights or imposing my new enthusiasms, helpful and good though these may be to me. Sometimes I forget Paul's background and his way of looking at things.

Although I may have opened a few windows for Paul, I know I cannot change the habits of thinking and feeling he has acquired through eight decades of living. And I must be careful not to manipulate this person who cannot verbally challenge me nor argue with me. My parents have not traveled my road of growth and experience; in their day and time, they traveled their own roads. I wish I knew more of their journeys, but in fact, I know as little of theirs as they know of mine.

Thus, I am trying to listen more, to understand, to interpret, to be an occasional catalyst for a new friendship or a new idea, to innovate, to receive information, and sometimes to respond. This, of course, is the stuff of true communication.

I, Too, Am Vulnerable

Today's news is frightening. International tensions of every kind threaten peace and equilibrium. I read about a future in which the trust funds of Social Security may be exhausted, about a world in which the building of schools must give way to the building of housing for increasing numbers of the elderly, most of whom may be women.

I realize that I, too, am growing old.

I wonder if my children will have to become parents to me. They have no such obligation, of course. Nevertheless, I want them to know some of my wishes for my own latter days. I do not wish heroic measures to be used to extend my life if it has become a mere existence. They should understand my wishes regarding the time of my death, and how I feel about disability if that should intervene.

I must begin to do some things for myself, looking ahead not only to retirement but also to my own death.

If I had to spend a lot of time in front of a television set (heaven forbid!), I understand enough about sports to enjoy watching them. Hockey is the exception, however, because I don't know the rules. I ought to learn them now.

I want to get my files in order. I don't want someone else to have to wade through reams of carbon copies and boxes of slides and photographic negatives, wondering what to save and what to discard. That's something I must begin to do soon.

I hope Carolyn and I will yet be able to see those places we've read and dreamed about. If God wills it, if savings hold out, and if inflation doesn't devour us all, we will. If this doesn't come to pass, we have already been blessed with an enormous amount of travel, so we'll just relax and remember.

Of course, I must not assume too much. Unless we die together in an accident or a disaster, it's likely that one of us will survive the other. And there is the specter of institutionalization. Neither of us possesses some ironclad guarantee that all will be well and serene.

Within the framework of my own vulnerability, I can only hope and trust the God I have followed. I hope I will be given the grace to continue to think, to read, and to write. If dependency comes, I hope it will be brief and not a burden to anyone. And in the process of caring for Paul and Anna with Carolyn beside me, as well as in the writing of this book, I hope I have learned something I can apply to my own life.

Returning to the Source

Our Judeo-Christian tradition commands us to honor father and mother (see Ex. 20:12, Eph. 6:2).

The psalmist cries out, "Do not cast me off in the time of old age..." (Ps. 71:9).

How can we deal with the commandment and the cry?

Love is the answer. The apostle Paul affirmed that love is the greatest of virtues, surpassing even faith and hope. I know we cannot will to love; we cannot force the emotion. However, we can determine for ourselves how our love will be lived out and expressed.

"Love is patient and kind..." Paul wrote to the Corinthian Christians (1 Cor. 13:4). But it isn't easy to be patient with an invalid or handicapped parent when weeks become months, and months become years.

Frustration builds and sometimes explodes into anger. Horror stories about abuse of parents are beginning to appear more frequently.

Perhaps Carolyn and I have had it easier than most couples facing this responsibility. Each of us has a parent who needs our love and care. We can lean on each other, sharing the burden and not blaming the other for the change this care imposes upon our daily life-style and our marriage.

But I must confess to flashes of irritation and anger. I could not understand why Anna could not find and use the bathroom just outside her door. I still get upset with Paul when he forgets, or sometimes refuses, to use the grab bars I placed so strategically to help him. And sometimes Carolyn is affected in this crossfire of frustration.

Patience can dissipate quickly when almost every visit to Anna includes digging out dirt and excrement from under her fingernails. I can become weary in well-doing when the doing means attaching a catheter to my father-in-law every night.

The Magic of Love

Love is patient and kind.

I have to remember these characteristics and demonstrate them. It was necessary to do this as our children were growing up, two of them in that strange and turbulent decade of the sixties. The words of the art song "Plaisir d'Amour" (Égide Martini, 1741-1816) so often seemed poignantly accurate: "The joys of love endure but for a day, The pains of true loving throughout a lifetime stay." It was easy then to say, "Act your age!" Later I wondered which age I had in mind—child, adolescent, or young adult?

My parents now act in ways that reflect their age. I wish their deterioration were not so severe, but I must be patient as they now act out their real age.

Good parenting has never meant forcing children to be extensions of their parents; rather, it means to model or illustrate the values and insights that will help children become responsible citizens and parents themselves. In the new parenting role we must sometimes assume for our own parents, we should also provide and model the care and security we gave our children. But our parents still must be allowed the privilege of being themselves and be given the honor and respect they still deserve.

I've always considered myself a rather generous person. But I also know I am a perfectionist who feels comfortable with schedules when they are kept and who prefers to solve problems rather than analyze them. It is difficult to be kind when one is rigid and it is almost impossible to be patient.

Reviewing the past six years of my life with Paul and Anna, I hope I have been kind and I think I am becoming more patient. At least I am more flexible.

It would be conveniently pious to say that the changes have come as I have learned to do the demanding things for my parents "as unto the Lord." Intellectually, I know we perform a service to Christ as we help those in need and in pain; I may even have thought this from time to time. Emotionally, however, I must declare that I do not picture Christ as I comb Anna's hair or adjust Paul's tie.

My "New" Parents

I have come to a new perception of Paul and Anna. As we children grow older, we see and understand our parents in new ways. That is part of maturing. The process for me has simply continued longer than I expected.

Ours was a strict, rigid family. We were Eastern European by background, polite, predictable, and not really close. We didn't embrace each other, and we wondered about those who did. We kissed only perfunctorily and rarely.

As an only child, much was expected of me—particularly in "Christian service." After all, my father was a minister and a missionary. At the age of five I memorized Scripture under the threat and use of a belt, usually administered by Anna; I learned a verse for each letter of the alphabet. At age seven I began to play the portable pump organ at street meetings. At age twelve I was pushed into a pulpit as a boy preacher.

That's a sampling of the emotional baggage I have had to discard.

I no longer see my mother as I saw her at age five, seven, or twelve. I see her now as a person who was herself pushed into situations and performances for which she was not prepared and about which she had her own fears and misgivings. I see her now as a person who was denied the affection she needed—first as an orphan and later by her husband and son.

I'm trying now to make up for the lack of affection. I have come to realize the necessity for tactile expression of affection for Anna. I hold her hand. I massage her back. I wash her face and hands, no longer with exasperation but because it is necessary. I kiss her before I leave. I'm not sure how much this means to her. Sometimes I think that touching may be the only way we communicate anything now. But I know this new dimension has taught me much, and I find I am touching many more of Anna's older friends, and I see how warmly they respond.

And what about Paul?

I've mentioned that I saw my own father more as a grandfather than as a father; he died when I was twenty-four, two weeks shy of his own sixty-eighth birthday. I've known Paul for more than thirty years—longer than I knew my own father. I've shared much with Paul during these three decades. He's become a father to me, and I think I've become the son he never had—often an argumentative, obstreperous son!

Paul has been pretty rigid himself—in theology, missionary strategy, family relationships, and politics. His daughters never challenged him. I did many times before his stroke, and often we found it possible to end such discussions in laughter rather than anger.

Things are different now with his inability to speak and to respond. I don't argue with Paul, but I do become irritated and angry when I feel he has needlessly endangered himself. Sometimes he has tried to walk without assistance. At the nursing home he sometimes forgets or refuses to use the call button for help and was found on the floor twice. At such times I've exploded, then explained, and finally apologized. Paul will often wave his hand, smile his half smile, and say what sounds like, "It's all right." In those moments I have experienced Paul's forgiveness and we can begin again.

I'm sure that in caring for Paul I am caring for my own father, who died too soon and whom I knew so little. I'm sure I'm also doing some of the things I wish I could do for Anna.

In trying to be patient and kind, I do so not so much "as unto the Lord" as I do simply for two people whom I love and who are my parents. In large measure, I do it for myself because I have a need that must be met.

I've written about the "new" parents in my life. There is also a new me.

Love Must Be Real

The apostle Paul wrote to the Christians in Rome, "Let love be genuine . . ." (Rom. 12:9). Let it be sincere, not artificial. Don't pretend, and don't try to fake it.

Paul Young's mind still works; he understands. Anna doesn't. But I think they both sense the authenticity of our love.

This business of parenting parents—facing and making decisions for those we love—will be easier if we remember that genuine love is patient, kind, honest, and realistic. Sometimes the expression of this love may not appear to be loving, especially when we must weigh long-term needs against the short term. Hard decisions have to be made for the good of our parents and ourselves.

We do not need to carry a burden of guilt throughout our lives if we remember and practice the criteria of love.

Let There Be Joy!

The apostle Paul wrote, "Rejoice in the Lord always. . . . Let all men know your forbearance . . . " (Phil. 4:4,5). He had more than his share of woe, but he believed difficulty and depression could be overcome.

Sister Corita says, "Laughter is a sign of hope. We are saved and we can afford to laugh once in a while."

I was washing Anna's hands one day when her roommate, Mrs. Williams, a kind and aware person, lent me a towel. In trying to keep Anna calm, I suddenly thought of an old kindergarten song and began to sing: "This is the way we wash our hands!"

Mrs. Williams picked it up, then so did Olga across the hall. Soon several of us were boisterously singing the old ditty. Anna didn't sing, but she was beaming and playing with the warm water. When we were through, Mrs. Williams said, in all seriousness: "Mr. Gillies, that was nice! How do you remember all of those old songs?"

Anna doesn't get the point of jokes anymore, but she'll listen to a story now and then. She likes pictures and color. She likes to watch other people, especially children, and she smiles easily and frequently.

Paul always loved to tell stories, and he still enjoys a good joke. We cut out cartoons and put these on his wall. "Family Circus" is a current favorite, and he enjoys showing these to his friends. It's delightful to hear his deep rumble of laughter.

A sense of humor, the gift of laughter, and an atmosphere of joy make life so much easier for Anna and Paul, and for us. I must not take myself too seriously, and I dare not take Anna and Paul too seriously.

How Should We Pray?

Jesus encourages us to pray for God's will on earth, for daily bread, for deliverance from evil, and to ask in order to receive.

A great promise is found in Psalm 91:15: "When he calls to me, I will answer him; I will be with him in trouble, I will rescue him and honor him."

The next verse intrigues me: "With long life I will satisfy him, and show him my salvation."

Should I pray for long life for Paul and for Anna? Or should I ask the Lord to take them to be with Him?

Anna is marking time. Life has lost all meaning for her. I do believe she will be happier in a new existence. Paul, on the other hand, is still aware of life. He still has many concerns for family members, for colleagues on mission fields, and for work and ministry yet to be completed. Paul's important ministry today is one of intercessory prayer. Should I pray that it should end, for my own convenience? No, I want God's will for both of them.

Since I do not know, then, how to pray, I am grateful for Romans 8:26: "Likewise the Spirit helps us in our weakness; for we do not know how to pray as we ought, but the Spirit himself intercedes for us with sighs too deep for words."

I pray for Carolyn and for myself, that we may be given health, patience, wisdom, and the ability to express our love.

I pray for Anna and for Paul, that God's Spirit may so surround them that they will always feel secure in His love.

And I pray for those who care for Anna and for Paul, that they too may be given patience, wisdom, and the ability to express *their* love.

A Day and a Night in the Life of a "New" Parent

It was Sunday, and we brought Paul into town and church. In the transfer from car seat to wheelchair, Paul did not stand fully erect nor take the usual step backward. I wrenched my back trying to keep Paul's 185 pounds upright while I shoved the wheelchair sideways, closer to Paul, with my foot.

Carolyn and I had been talking about resuming long-term care for Paul in our home. As I nursed my lower back pain, I pondered whether I would still have the physical and emotional stamina to respond lovingly and competently.

Paul was tired that morning, and slept through most of the service. I wondered whether these kinds of efforts really made that much difference to him.

Later that same Sunday, I spent an hour with my mother. She had been restless during the vespers, chattering away to herself and pushing against the brakes of her wheelchair. I had felt she needed the opportunity to listen to the singing and reading, that some structure would be helpful. Now I wondered whether I was placing too great a value upon such reluctant participation. Was the service really helpful to her? I didn't think her presence and chatter was helping the vespers leader. Could we find other ways to better use this time together?

In the meantime, Carolyn had returned Paul to Trinity Home in Round Rock. She joined me and Anna, and we sat together until it was time to take Anna to the dining room for her supper.

I had brought two felt pens and some paper. I asked Anna to write her name. She smiled and scrawled some squiggly lines. I drew a circle and put in two eyes. She had entertained me this way when I was a toddler. I asked her to put in a mouth—which she did first with a straight line, turning it up on one side, and extending the other side beyond the face. It looked like an enormous smile, and Anna beamed at her work. Then she doodled, drawing what appeared to be borders around the page. Ten minutes had passed, and so had her interest. We proceeded to the dining room.

Most of that night was restless and sleepless for Carolyn and me. Carolyn was ill with severe lower intestinal pain. I was aware of the discomfort of my lower back. Also, the chest pains that always come when I am very tired had returned; they are probably psychosomatic.

Doubts and fears began to crowd into my mind. Could Carolyn and I continue to cope with the needs of our parents? And what if our parents should outlive us?

When sleep finally came, I dreamed about Anna. There had been some sort of picnic, arranged by the nursing home. Carolyn and I were present but were obligated to leave early; the nursing staff assured us everything would be fine. Later, I returned to check on Anna, but she wasn't in the nursing home—and no one knew where she was.

I found her in the picnic area, *standing* in front of her wheelchair. She was swaying slowly as she stood. She looked terribly emaciated and dirty, as though she had fallen and played in the dirt. She did not recognize me. She stood bewildered, staring blankly into space. She looked so forlorn and abandoned.

As I lay awake, I realized that Anna was worrying me more than Paul, although there was very little we could do now for Anna. I glanced at Carolyn, sleeping beside me. We have survived these years in remarkably good fashion, but we both share scars from the experience.

Why do we bother?

Paul is often morose. Anna is detached. We certainly do not struggle to provide loving care for praise or even thanks; we get very little of this from Paul, and none from Anna.

In the quiet of that dark night, it seemed to me that we had been given a gift—the possibility and opportunity to serve two people who need us. Somehow, through all of this, all things will work together for our good (Rom. 8:28).

We Live With Hope

Who shall separate us from the love of Christ? Shall tribulation, or distress, or persecution, or famine, or nakedness, or peril, or sword?

. . . No, in all these things we are more than conquerors through him who loved us. For I am sure that neither death, nor life, nor angels, nor principalities, nor things present, nor things to come, nor powers, nor height, nor depth, *nor anything else in all creation* [doesn't that include the effects of stroke and senility?], will be able to separate us from the love of God in Christ Jesus our Lord (Rom. 8:35,37-39, italics mine).

Karl Barth, the great Swiss theologian, was once asked at Princeton Seminary how he would summarize his faith. His reply shocked some of the seminarians: "Jesus loves me, this I know, for the Bible tells me so!"

There's a verse of Anna Warner's old Sunday school song that isn't often sung, but it applies beautifully to our parents who are ill or handicapped.

> Jesus loves me, loves me still,
> Though I'm very weak and ill;
> From His shining throne on high,
> Comes to watch me where I lie.

I need that reassurance, too.

Afterword

Many months elapse between the writing of a book and its appearance. In the case of this book, more than a year has passed.

What has happened during that year?

Paul is again living with us.

We have found another aide who is able to give us twenty hours a week in the mornings. Carolyn and I will try to manage the rest of the time between us. We are agreed that we will take time off for evening events, separately or together, and for occasional weekend breaks. And we will secure other help so we can do this.

It troubled me to read the sign the county officials put up just in front of Trinity Home: DEAD END.

There were many sad farewells the day Paul left the home. After everything was packed and we were in the car, I asked Paul if he had any second thoughts. He shook his head and pointed a finger upwards. I thought for a moment and asked, "You mean, the next move you want to make is 'up there'?" He smiled and nodded yes.

We've arranged the furniture in Paul's old room and took up the shag rug so he can move about more easily in his wheelchair. We want to preserve some of the new independence he achieved in the nursing home.

We think we can provide a more consistent level of creature care for him, having learned from our previous experience.

Anna remains in Capitol City Nursing Home and will continue to require the level of skilled care she receives there.

Just the other day when I was helping her with her lunch, she suddenly smiled and reached over to touch my cheek and then to feel my sport shirt. Then she took her half slice of whole wheat bread, broke it in two, and offered me a piece.

For a moment I, too, saw the Lord in the breaking of bread.

Address List

Action for Independent Maturity, 1909 K St., NW, Washington, DC 20049
American Aging Association, University of Nebraska Medical Center, Omaha, NE 68105.
American Association of Homes for the Aging, 1050 17th St., NW, Washington, DC 20036.
American Association of Retired Persons, 215 Long Beach Blvd., Long Beach, CA 90801.
American Bible Society, 1865 Broadway, New York, NY 10023.
American Cancer Society, 219 E. 42nd St., New York, NY 10021.
American Diabetes Association, 18 E. 48th St., New York, NY 10017.
American Foundation for the Blind, Inc., 15 W. 16th St., New York, NY 10011.
American Geriatrics Society, 10 Columbus Circle, New York, NY 10011.
American Health Care Association, 2500 15th St., NW, Washington, DC 20015.
American Heart Association, 44 W. 23rd St., New York, NY 10010.
American Lung Association, 1740 Broadway, New York, NY 10019.
American Medical Association, 535 N. Dearborn St., Chicago, IL 60610.
American Occupational Therapy Association, Inc., 6000 Executive Blvd., Rockville, MD 20852.
American Physical Therapy Association, 1740 Broadway, New York, NY 10019.
American Red Cross, 17th and D Sts., NW, Washington, DC 20006.
Andrus Gerontology Center, University of Southern California, Los Angeles, CA 90007. (Dr. Ethel Andrus was the founder of AARP.)
Association of Rehabilitation Facilities, 5530 Wisconsin Ave., NW, Washington, DC 20015.
Center for the Study of Aging and Human Development, Duke University, Durham, NC 27710.
Concern for Dying (an educational council), 250 W. 57th St., New York, NY 10107.
Continental Association of Funeral and Memorial Societies, 1828 L St., NW, Washington, DC 20036.
Elderhostel, 100 Boylston St., Suite 200, Boston, MA 02116.
Episcopal Society for Ministry on Aging, Inc., R.D. #1, Box 28, Milford, NJ 08848.
Family Service Association of America, 44 W. 23rd St., New York, NY 10010.
Gerontological Society, 1 Dupont Circle, Washington, DC 20036.
Gray Panthers, 3635 Chestnut St., Philadelphia, PA 19104.

Hogg Foundation for Mental Health, The University of Texas, Austin, TX 78712.

Homemakers' Home and Health Care Services, 3651 Van Rick Drive, Kalamazoo, MI 49001.

Jewish Guild for the Blind, 15 W. 65th St., New York, NY 10023.

Living Bank, P. O. Box 6725, Houston, TX 77005.

Lutheran Braille Workers, Inc., Sight-Saving Division, 495 9th Ave., San Francisco, CA 94118.

Lutheran Tape Ministry, Box 125, Seward, NE 68434.

National Association for Mental Health, 1800 North Kent St., Arlington, VA 22209.

National Association for Visually Handicapped, 305 E. 24th St., New York, NY 10010.

National Association of the Deaf, 814 Thayer Ave., Silver Spring, MD 20910.

National Association of Hearing and Speech Agencies, 814 Thayer Ave., Silver Spring, MD 20910.

National Caucus on the Black Aged, 1730 M St., NW, Washington, DC 20036.

National Council on the Aging, Suite 504, 1828 L St., NW, Washington, DC 20036.

National Council for Homemaker-Home Health Aide Services, 67 Irving Place, New York, NY 10003.

National Council of Senior Citizens, 1511 K St., NW, Room 202, Washington, DC 20005.

National Interfaith Coalition on Aging, Inc., P. O. Box 1986, Indianapolis, IN 46206.

National Retired Teachers Association, 1901 K St., NW, Washington, D.C. 20036.

New Eyes for the Needy, Inc., Short Hills, NJ 07078.

Dr. Garland O'Quinn Jr., Physical Activity Consultant, P. O. Box 4548, Austin, TX 78765.

Pacific Garden Mission, 646 S. State St., Chicago, IL 60605.

Preventicare, Lawrence Frankel Foundation, Virginia and Brooks St., Charleston, WV 25301.

Reigner Recording Library, Union Theological Seminary, Richmond, VA 23227.

Unshackled! radio series (see *Pacific Garden Mission*).

U.S. Administration on Aging, 3303 C St., SW, HHS South, Washington, DC 20024. (Administers ten regional offices. Each state has its own Department, Office, or Commission on Aging, usually located in the state capital.)